The
Blackfeet

THE HISTORY & CULTURE of NATIVE AMERICANS

This book is dedicated to those who lost their lives in the
Bear River Massacre of 1870. –TJL

The Blackfeet
Copyright © 2011 by Infobase Learning

All rights reserved. No part of this book may be reproduced or utilized in any form or by any means, electronic or mechanical, including photocopying, recording, or by any information storage or retrieval systems, without permission in writing from the publisher. For information contact:

Chelsea House
An imprint of Infobase Learning
132 West 31st Street
New York, NY 10001

Library of Congress Cataloging-in-Publication Data
Lacey, Theresa Jensen.
    The Blackfeet / T. Jensen Lacey.
        p. cm. — (The history and culture of Native Americans)
    Includes bibliographical references and index.
    ISBN 978-1-60413-795-8 (hardcover)
    1. Siksika Indians—Juvenile literature. 2. Kainah Indians—Juvenile literature. 3. Piegan Indians—Juvenile literature. I. Title.
    E99.S54L33 2011
    978.004'97352—dc22   2010044827

Chelsea House books are available at special discounts when purchased in bulk quantities for businesses, associations, institutions, or sales promotions. Please call our Special Sales Department in New York at (212) 967-8800 or (800) 322-8755.

You can find Chelsea House on the World Wide Web at
http://www.infobaselearning.com

Text design by Lina Farinella
Cover design by Alicia Post
Composition by Newgen
Cover printed by Yurchak Printing, Landisville, Pa.
Book printed and bound by Yurchak Printing, Landisville, Pa.
Date printed: June 2011
Printed in the United States of America

10 9 8 7 6 5 4 3 2 1
This book is printed on acid-free paper.

All links and Web addresses were checked and verified to be correct at the time of publication. Because of the dynamic nature of the Web, some addresses and links may have changed since publication and may no longer be valid.

3 1350 00306 2959

THE HISTORY & CULTURE of NATIVE AMERICANS

The
Blackfeet

T. JENSEN LACEY

Series Editor
PAUL C. ROSIER

CHELSEA HOUSE
An Infobase Learning Company

Contents

Foreword
by Paul C. Rosier

Native American words, phrases, and tribal names are embedded in the very geography of the United States—in the names of creeks, rivers, lakes, cities, and states, including Alabama, Connecticut, Iowa, Kansas, Illinois, Missouri, Oklahoma, and many others. Yet Native Americans remain the most misunderstood ethnic group in the United States. This is a result of limited coverage of Native American history in middle schools, high schools, and colleges; poor coverage of contemporary Native American issues in the news media; and stereotypes created by Hollywood movies, sporting events, and TV shows.

Two newspaper articles about American Indians caught my eye in recent months. Paired together, they provide us with a good introduction to the experiences of American Indians today: first, how they are stereotyped and turned into commodities; and second, how they see themselves being a part of the United States and of the wider world. (Note: I use the terms *Native Americans* and *American Indians* interchangeably; both terms are considered appropriate.)

In the first article, "Humorous Souvenirs to Some, Offensive Stereotypes to Others," written by Carol Berry in *Indian Country Today*, I read that tourist shops in Colorado were selling "souvenir" T-shirts portraying American Indians as drunks. "My Indian name is Runs with Beer," read one T-shirt offered in Denver. According to the article, the T-shirts are "the kind of stereotype-reinforcing products also seen in nearby Boulder, Estes Park, and likely other Colorado communities, whether as part of the tourism trade or as everyday merchandise." No other ethnic group in the United States is stereotyped in such a public fashion. In addition, Native people are used to sell a range of consumer goods, including the Jeep Cherokee, Red Man chewing tobacco, Land O'Lakes butter, and other items that either objectify or insult them, such as cigar store Indians. As importantly, non-Indians learn about American Indian history and culture through sports teams such as the Atlanta Braves, Cleveland Indians, Florida State Seminoles, or Washington Redskins, whose name many American Indians consider a racist insult; dictionaries define *redskin* as a "disparaging" or "offensive" term for American Indians. When fans in Atlanta do their "tomahawk chant" at Braves baseball games, they perform two inappropriate and related acts: One, they perpetuate a stereotype of American Indians as violent; and two, they tell a historical narrative that covers up the violent ways that Georgians treated the Cherokee during the Removal period of the 1830s.

The second article, written by Melissa Pinion-Whitt of the San Bernardino *Sun* addressed an important but unknown dimension of Native American societies that runs counter to the irresponsible and violent image created by products and sporting events. The article, "San Manuels Donate $1.7 M for Aid to Haiti," described a Native American community that had sent aid to Haiti after it was devastated in January 2010 by an earthquake that killed more than 200,000 people, injured hundreds of thousands more, and destroyed the Haitian capital. The San Manuel Band of Mission Indians in California donated $1.7 million to help relief efforts in Haiti; San Manuel children held fund-raisers to collect additional donations. For the San Manuel Indians it was nothing new; in 2007 they had donated $1 million to help Sudanese refugees in Darfur. San Manuel also contributed $700,000 to relief efforts following Hurricane Katrina and Hurricane Rita, and donated $1 million in 2007 for wildfire recovery in Southern California.

Such generosity is consistent with many American Indian nations' cultural practices, such as the "give-away," in which wealthy tribal members give to the needy, and the "potlatch," a winter gift-giving ceremony and feast tradition shared by tribes in the

Pacific Northwest. And it is consistent with historical accounts of American Indians' generosity. For example, in 1847 Cherokee and Choctaw, who had recently survived their forced march on a "Trail of Tears" from their homelands in the American South to present-day Oklahoma, sent aid to Irish families after reading of the potato famine, which created a similar forced migration of Irish. A Cherokee newspaper editorial, quoted in Christine Kinealy's *The Great Irish Famine: Impact, Ideology, and Rebellion,* explained that the Cherokee "will be richly repaid by the consciousness of having done a good act, by the moral effect it will produce abroad." During and after World War II, nine Pueblo communities in New Mexico offered to donate food to the hungry in Europe, after Pueblo army veterans told stories of suffering they had witnessed while serving in the United States armed forces overseas. Considering themselves a part of the wider world, Native people have reached beyond their borders, despite their own material poverty, to help create a peaceful world community.

American Indian nations have demonstrated such generosity within the United States, especially in recent years. After the terrorist attacks of September 11, 2001, the Lakota Sioux in South Dakota offered police officers and emergency medical personnel to New York City to help with relief efforts; Indian nations across the country sent millions of dollars to help the victims of the attacks. As an editorial in the *Native American Times* newspaper explained on September 12, 2001, "American Indians love this country like no other. . . . Today, we are all New Yorkers."

Indeed, Native Americans have sacrificed their lives in defending the United States from its enemies in order to maintain their right to be both American and Indian. As the volumes in this series tell us, Native Americans patriotically served as soldiers (including as "code talkers") during World War I and World War II, as well as during the Korean War, the Vietnam War, and, after 9/11, the wars in Afghanistan and Iraq. Native soldiers, men and women, do so today by the tens of thousands because they believe in America, an

America that celebrates different cultures and peoples. Sgt. Leonard Gouge, a Muscogee Creek, explained it best in an article in *Cherokee News Path* in discussing his post-9/11 army service. He said he was willing to serve his country abroad because "by supporting the American way of life, I am preserving the Indian way of life."

This new Chelsea House series has two main goals. The first is to document the rich diversity of American Indian societies and the ways their cultural practices and traditions have evolved over time. The second goal is to provide the reader with coverage of the complex relationships that have developed between non-Indians and Indians over the past several hundred years. This history helps to explain why American Indians consider themselves both American and Indian and why they see preserving this identity as a strength of the American way of life, as evidence to the rest of the world that America is a champion of cultural diversity and religious freedom. By exploring Native Americans' cultural diversity and their contributions to the making of the United States, these volumes confront the stereotypes that paint all American Indians as the same and portray them as violent; as "drunks," as those Colorado T-shirts do; or as rich casino owners, as many news accounts do.

*　*　*

Each of the 14 volumes in this series is written by a scholar who shares my conviction that young adult readers are both fascinated by Native American history and culture and have not been provided with sufficient material to properly understand the diverse nature of this complex history and culture. The authors themselves represent a varied group that includes university teachers and professional writers, men and women, and Native and non-Native. To tell these fascinating stories, this talented group of scholars has examined an incredible variety of sources, both the primary sources that historical actors have created and the secondary sources that historians and anthropologists have written to make sense of the past.

Although the 14 Indian nations (also called tribes and communities) selected for this series have different histories and cultures,
they all share certain common experiences. In particular, they had
to face an American empire that spread westward in the eighteenth
and nineteenth centuries, causing great trauma and change for all
Native people in the process. Because each volume documents
American Indians' experiences dealing with powerful non-Indian
institutions and ideas, I outline below the major periods and features of federal Indian policy making in order to provide a frame
of reference for complex processes of change with which American
Indians had to contend. These periods—Assimilation, Indian New
Deal, Termination, Red Power, and Self-determination—and specific acts of legislation that define them—in particular the General
Allotment Act, the Indian Reorganization Act, and the Indian Self-
determination and Education Assistance Act—will appear in all the
volumes, especially in the latter chapters.

In 1851, the commissioner of the federal Bureau of Indian
Affairs (BIA) outlined a three-part program for subduing American Indians militarily and assimilating them into the United States:
concentration, domestication, and incorporation. In the first phase,
the federal government waged war with the American Indian
nations of the American West in order to "concentrate" them on
reservations, away from expanding settlements of white Americans
and immigrants. Some American Indian nations experienced terrible violence in resisting federal troops and state militia; others
submitted peacefully and accepted life on a reservation. During
this phase, roughly from the 1850s to the 1880s, the U.S. government signed hundreds of treaties with defeated American Indian
nations. These treaties "reserved" to these American Indian nations
specific territory as well as the use of natural resources. And they
provided funding for the next phase of "domestication."

During the domestication phase, roughly the 1870s to the early
1900s, federal officials sought to remake American Indians in the
mold of white Americans. Through the Civilization Program, which

actually started with President Thomas Jefferson, federal officials sent religious missionaries, farm instructors, and teachers to the newly created reservations in an effort to "kill the Indian to save the man," to use a phrase of that time. The ultimate goal was to extinguish American Indian cultural traditions and turn American Indians into Christian yeoman farmers. The most important piece of legislation in this period was the General Allotment Act (or Dawes Act), which mandated that American Indian nations sell much of their territory to white farmers and use the proceeds to farm on what was left of their homelands. The program was a failure, for the most part, because white farmers got much of the best arable land in the process. Another important part of the domestication agenda was the federal boarding school program, which required all American Indian children to attend schools to further their rejection of Indian ways and the adoption of non-Indian ways. The goal of federal reformers, in sum, was to incorporate (or assimilate) American Indians into American society as individual citizens and not as groups with special traditions and religious practices.

During the 1930s some federal officials came to believe that American Indians deserved the right to practice their own religion and sustain their identity as Indians, arguing that such diversity made America stronger. During the Indian New Deal period of the 1930s, BIA commissioner John Collier devised the Indian Reorganization Act (IRA), which passed in 1934, to give American Indian nations more power, not less. Not all American Indians supported the IRA, but most did. They were eager to improve their reservations, which suffered from tremendous poverty that resulted in large measure from federal policies such as the General Allotment Act.

Some federal officials opposed the IRA, however, and pushed for the assimilation of American Indians in a movement called Termination. The two main goals of Termination advocates, during the 1950s and 1960s, were to end (terminate) the federal reservation system and American Indians' political sovereignty derived from treaties and to relocate American Indians from rural reservations to urban areas. These coercive federal assimilation policies in turn generated resistance from Native Americans, including young activists who helped to create the so-called Red Power era of the 1960s and 1970s, which coincided with the African-American civil rights movement. This resistance led to the federal government's rejection of Termination policies in 1970. And in 1975 the U.S. Congress passed the Indian Self-determination and Education Assistance Act, which made it the government's policy to support American Indians' right to determine the future of their communities. Congress then passed legislation to help American Indian nations to improve reservation life; these acts strengthened American Indians' religious freedom, political sovereignty, and economic opportunity.

All American Indians, especially those in the western United States, were affected in some way by the various federal policies described above. But it is important to highlight the fact that each American Indian community responded in different ways to these pressures for change, both the detribalization policies of assimilation and the retribalization policies of self-determination. There is no one group of "Indians." American Indians were and still are a very diverse group. Some embraced the assimilation programs of the federal government and rejected the old traditions; others refused to adopt non-Indian customs or did so selectively, on their own terms. Most American Indians, as I noted above, maintain a dual identity of American and Indian.

Today, there are more than 550 American Indian (and Alaska Natives) nations recognized by the federal government. They have a legal and political status similar to states, but they have special rights and privileges that are the result of congressional acts and the hundreds of treaties that still govern federal-Indian relations today. In July 2008, the total population of American Indians (and Alaska Natives) was 4.9 million, representing about 1.6 percent of the United States population. The state with the highest number of American Indians is California, followed by Oklahoma, home to the Cherokee (the largest American Indian nation in terms of population), and then Arizona, home to the Navajo (the second-largest American Indian nation). All told, roughly half of the American Indian population lives in urban areas; the other half lives on reservations and in other rural parts of the country. Like all their fellow American citizens, American Indians pay federal taxes, obey federal laws, and vote in federal, state, and local elections; they also participate in the democratic processes of their American Indian nations, electing judges, politicians, and other civic officials.

This series on the history and culture of Native Americans celebrates their diversity and differences as well as the ways they have strengthened the broader community of America. Ronnie Lupe, the chairman of the White Mountain Apache government in Arizona, once addressed questions from non-Indians as to "why Indians serve the United States with such distinction and honor?" Lupe, a Korean War veteran, answered those questions during the Gulf War of 1991–1992, in which Native American soldiers served to protect the independence of the Kuwaiti people. He explained in "Chairman's Corner" in *The Fort Apache Scout* that "our loyalty to the United States goes beyond our need to defend our home and reservation lands. . . . Only a few in this country really understand that the indigenous people are a national treasure. Our values have the potential of creating the social, environmental, and spiritual healing that could make this country truly great."

—Paul C. Rosier
Associate Professor of History
Villanova University

The Migration
of the Blackfeet
People

When Christopher Columbus "discovered" what was to become known as America in 1492, Europeans hailed his achievement. This era of discovery led by Columbus's explorations, however, marked the beginning of centuries of tragic events in the lives of Native Americans. The people living then in the so-called civilized world did not begin to consider that millions of people already dwelled on the continent Columbus had inadvertently stumbled upon. In the time known as the Pre-Columbian Era, the people now called Native Americans had their own cultures, traditions, ways of life, and deities. They had a rich existence and a vibrant history. The Blackfeet people are a part of that group.

"American Indian culture," the Web site of the group of people collectively and officially known as the Blackfoot Confederacy says, "has not only survived 150 years of intensive effort to eradicate it, it is once again flourishing and undergoing a rebirth, a revitalization." The Blackfeet call themselves, collectively, Niit-sítapi, which means "original people." The Blackfeet consist of three divisions: the Siksika (known as the Blackfeet proper); the Blood, or Kainah (Many Chiefs); and the Pikuni (The Poorly Dressed Ones), also known as the Piegan or Peigan. The Piegan are further divided into the Canadian North Piegan and the American South Piegan. Present-day Blackfeet reside in the Siksika, Kainah, and Piegan reserves in Alberta, Canada, but the majority of them live on the Blackfeet Reservation near Browning, Montana.

Blackfeet tribal member Wendy Running Crane mentioned the various names by which her people are called: "Refer to all the bands collectively as the Blackfoot Confederacy," she wrote in an e-mail, "as they don't call themselves Blackfeet on the Canadian side." She went on to add, "The Blackfeet Nation refers to our band only—the Amskapi Pikuni (South Piegans). North Piegans call themselves Pikaani Nation."

There are several different stories regarding how the Blackfeet came to be called by their name. Some say that the name came from the color of the soles of the moccasins worn by tribe members; the soles were darkened either with paint or by walking over burnt prairie grasses. Before the incursion of Anglo-Europeans, the term *Blackfeet* was meant only for the Siksika division. Since the three divisions are culturally and linguistically related, however, *Blackfeet* will be used to refer to all the divisions unless otherwise specified. Sometimes, even on the official tribal Web site, the Blackfeet are also referred to as the Blackfoot; for the purposes of this book, however, we will continue to use Blackfeet.

The language shared by the three divisions is known as Algonquian. The Algonquian family of languages includes those spoken by indigenous peoples from Labrador to the Carolinas and westward into the Great Plains. The term *Algonquian* also refers to the people who share this language, according to *Merriam-Webster's Collegiate Dictionary*.

AN ORAL HISTORY

Language brings people together, helps preserve their cultural identity, and is their primary method of communication. As far back as recorded history goes, language and culture have been intertwined. The Blackfeet people kept their history and traditions alive through songs, stories, and ceremonies, passed down from one generation to the next. They don't consider their stories to be myths or legends.

Leroy Little Bear, who contributed to Marie Battiste's book *Reclaiming Indigenous Voice and Vision,* was emphatic yet eloquent in what he had to say about the European worldview clashing with the aboriginal cultures' worldviews and ways of passing on history in the oral tradition. In his chapter entitled "Jagged Worldviews Colliding," he pointed out the vastly different ways Europeans thought of history, time, and nature, which were the polar opposite of the beliefs of the Blackfeet. While Europeans regarded Blackfeet oral traditions and the passing down of stories as "legends" or "myths," these stories were and are as real to the Blackfeet people as what has been written in books by Europeans about their own history.

If you were to ask modern Blackfeet how they came to arrive in their part of the world, they would probably look at you in amazement and tell you that they have always been there. Anthropologists and scientists, however, say that long ago there was an immense migration of people to the continent now known as North America.

The most commonly accepted scientific theory of how the Blackfeet and other Native Americans came to arrive here is known as the Bering Strait Theory. Scientists believe that long ago a very slender strip of land connected Asia to North America in the Bering Sea, which separates what are now known as Alaska and Siberia. They claim further that this migration lasted at least 1,000 years. While some scientists, including geneticists, say that the migration took place approximately 30,000 years ago, others insist that it happened much earlier, as far back as 50,000 years ago. The Blackfeet Nation Web site says in its tribal timeline that, as far back as 8500 B.C., their ancestors developed communal hunting techniques, but nothing is mentioned about their arrival on this continent. This is because, as mentioned earlier, they believe they have always been here.

Whether people believe the scientists' theories or choose to consider that the Blackfeet people were always on this continent, the Blackfeet at one time were living farther north than they are now. After the Bering Strait migration, anthropologists believe that the ancestors of the Blackfeet traveled south, then turned east and north. They settled in what is now the northwestern United States and southeastern Canada; due to their location, the Blackfeet are among the group of tribes known collectively as the Plains Indians. This group includes the Sioux, Crow, Kiowa, Arikara, Pawnee, Nez Perce, Cheyenne, Cree, and Gros Ventre.

The Plains Indians were often at war with each other but sometimes traded together as well. Even though they share a certain geographic area, they should not be grouped together as if they are one people. While they may share aspects of a particular culture or way of life, the Plains Indians should never be considered a culturally and linguistically homogenous group. The Blackfeet were and are as different from, say, the Cree, as an English person is from an American; to group any of these tribes together reveals a lack of cultural awareness.

ON THE PLAINS

Once the Blackfeet settled on the Great Plains, they became, as artist George Catlin called them, "the most powerful tribe of Indians on the continent." Before the introduction of the horse, they probably lived on the Plains in the northwestern area of what is now the province of Saskatchewan in Canada. They were also probably hunter-gatherers. There is no evidence that they cultivated any crops (with the exception of tobacco). Once they acquired the

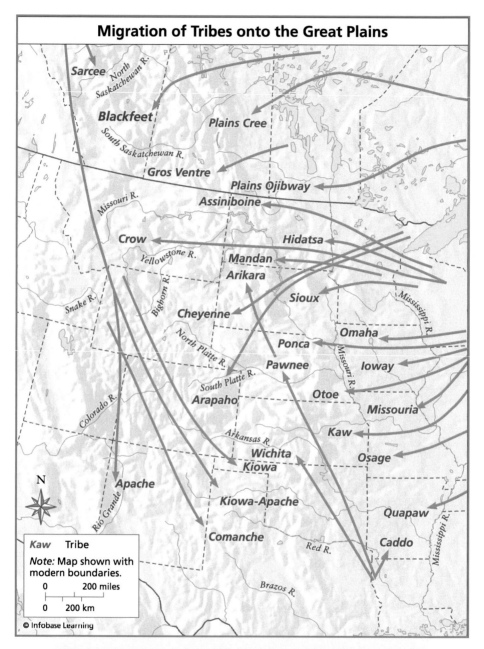

Migration of Tribes onto the Great Plains

While the Blackfeet believe that they have always lived in North America, researchers and scientists say that they, like other indigenous groups, traveled over the Bering Strait in prehistoric times and eventually settled in the Great Plains.

horse from Spanish explorers, they settled in the northwest corner of the Great Plains, rapidly displacing other tribes. With the horse, they became adroit hunters, invaluable as allies and dreaded as enemies.

The area of North America where the Blackfeet settled had to be a challenging environment, to say the least. Making their home in the fertile foothills of the Rocky Mountains, the Blackfeet had a natural boundary to their territory, since the mountains provided them with protection from surprise attacks. Below the timber line of the Rockies, cedars, hemlocks, spruce, pine, and fir trees offered protection and food for all kinds of wild game. The valleys were also full of rich, dark soil and had an abundance of clear freshwater streams and creeks. This attracted, protected, and offered sustenance to a huge variety of wildlife, from several hundred species of birds to mink, deer, beaver, and fox; the plains were also filled with immense herds of buffalo. No one really knows how large these great herds were, but when the Lewis and Clark expedition came through the area in the early 1800s, the explorers were amazed that one herd took an entire day to cross a river.

The Rocky Mountains and Great Plains region, while being full of game and rich soil, also had extreme weather conditions. The Blackfeet called the Great Plains the "Sea of Grass." Weather could roll in without warning. One mid-afternoon might begin gentle and balmy; then violent prairie storms would overtake the unsuspecting hunter. Winds could become violent, with sudden gusts as forceful as a tornado. Winters were so extreme that early white settlers referred to them as "hells."

THE IMPORTANCE OF THE HORSE

One animal that aided the Blackfeet in not only surviving but also thriving in this challenging environment was the horse, which was named "Ponokaamiitaa," or "Elk Dog," because it did the work of a dog but was the size of an elk. The horse, which was not indigenous to this continent, was brought over by the Spanish

The Blackfeet relied on dogs to help them move heavy items and to hunt before Europeans introduced the horse to the North America. Acquiring horses changed the Blackfeet lifestyle, allowing them to hunt better and move faster.

explorers who first arrived here in the early 1500s. Before obtaining the horse, the Blackfeet people were obliged to hunt and travel on foot. Their territory, though, was vast, including an area of more than 780,000 square miles, or 2 million square kilometers (covering most of present-day Montana, Alberta, and Saskatchewan). To carry their burdens when moving camp over this immense region, the Blackfeet had depended upon their camp dogs. They attached a contraption called a *travois* to the dogs' backs, enabling the animals to do much of the work in moving the camp. (According to Wendy Running Crane, in their oral history, the Blackfeet call this period of time "The Dog Days." In an e-mail, she wrote, "To this day, the dog or 'li-mi-taa' is considered with respect for when he helped us.")

With the arrival of Spanish explorers, however, the lives of the Blackfeet and other Native Americans changed dramatically. Some anthropologists say that the Blackfeet acquired their first horses through a skirmish with some Shoshone warriors; others say that they did so through peaceful trade with the Flathead, Kootenai, and Nez Perce tribes. At any rate, most historians agree that the Blackfeet acquired the horse around 1730. The horse enabled them to roam farther and more rapidly in search of game and carry more meat and other provisions. Horses also became a new kind of status symbol for hunters and warriors alike: Now, they were no longer eking out an existence on the "Sea of Grass" but were in charge of their own destiny. For a warrior, owning a herd of horses was a sign of prosperity and his ability to provide for his wife and family. As such, the herd became an offering when a man was courting a bride.

One major reason to emphasize the arrival of the horse in the Blackfeet world is because it changed every aspect of their lives. They became semi-nomadic, as the horse allowed them to follow the great herds of buffalo roaming the Great Plains. The Blackfeet became known as excellent equestrians, and even children at a very young age were taught to ride. Blackfeet warriors and hunters became adept at riding at a full gallop, shooting an enemy or a buffalo while hanging from under the horse's neck. Artists such as Frederick Remington and George Catlin became famous for their paintings of this era; they traveled and lived among many Native American nations, including the Blackfeet. Their depictions of Blackfeet hunters and warriors in action are still famous today.

The horse allowed the population of the Blackfeet to grow and prosper; it also helped protect them against the encroachment of other Native American peoples, such as the Flathead, Kootenai, Cree, Chippewa, Shoshone, and Crow, as well as settlers coming

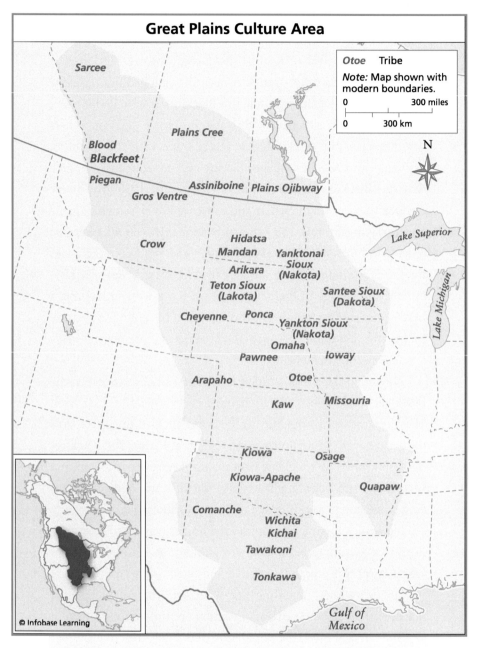

Great Plains Culture Area

Otoe Tribe

Note: Map shown with modern boundaries.

0 — 300 miles

0 — 300 km

N

Sarcee

Plains Cree

Blood

Blackfeet

Piegan

Gros Ventre

Assiniboine Plains Ojibway

Lake Superior

Crow

Hidatsa

Mandan

Arikara

Teton Sioux
(Lakota)

Yanktonai
Sioux
(Nakota)

Santee Sioux
(Dakota)

Lake Michigan

Cheyenne Ponca

Yankton Sioux
(Nakota)

Omaha

Ioway

Pawnee

Arapaho

Otoe

Kaw

Missouria

Kiowa

Osage

Kiowa-Apache

Quapaw

Comanche

Wichita
Kichai

Tawakoni

Tonkawa

Gulf of
Mexico

© Infobase Learning

This map shows the approximate locations of major tribes in the Great Plains Culture Area, including the Blackfeet. Farming tribes moved onto the plains from river valleys and woodlands to adopt a nomadic way of life dependent on the buffalo. A shared culture emerged from mingled tribal customs and a common way of life.

into their lands. In short, the horse transformed the entire world, and perspective, of the Blackfeet people.

CONTACT WITH EUROPEANS

It was only a matter of time before the Blackfeet would become exposed to other cultures. Although there are brief accounts of European explorers seeing Blackfeet around 1650, the first meaningful contact with an Anglo-European was with Henry Helsey of the Hudson's Bay Company in 1690 in Alberta, Canada. In roughly 1731, French Jesuits whom the Blackfeet people called "Black Robes" lived in their territory; later, around 1748, French fur trappers also appeared there. While other traders met the Blackfeet, the first person who probably had any success with them was Anthony Hendry. He was the first white man to stay with the Blackfeet, encamping with some Bloods in 1754 near present-day Red Deer in Alberta. Although the Blackfeet were not interested in trading, this contact was seen as a breakthrough. Finally, fur trader David Thompson wintered with the Piegan, and the Northwest Fur Trading Company began to trade with the Siksika and the Blood. Originally, the Blackfeet were reluctant to trade because they regarded the animals to be sacred beings. One reason they finally capitulated was because of the competition with their tribal Plains neighbors to acquire modern-day tools.

Before reservation life, the enemies of the Blackfeet were most commonly the Flathead, Kootenai, Cree, and especially the Crow. To a lesser extent they also fought the Shoshone and the Ute, taking horses and hostages; all these were tribes who shared the Great Plains and its bounty, however unwillingly, with the Blackfeet. There are accounts of Blackfeet warriors having tense encounters with the Crow and the Flathead, who had begun to lead fur traders and American explorers into Blackfeet country. The U.S. government would later take note of such enmity between Native nations and use this information to its advantage, sending out scouts from one tribe to track down other Native Americans who were wanted by the government.

As the Blackfeet fought against their tribal counterparts, they realized their competitors were gaining goods such as guns, supplies, and horses. The Blackfeet began to realize the futility of their resistance to trade with Anglo-Europeans. Such trade finally occurred around 1780, and the Blackfeet acquired much-needed goods, like guns and other weapons, metal tools, and ammunition, in exchange for the horses and mules they obtained in their raiding forays.

Perhaps the most vivid accounts of early contact with the Blackfeet were by members of the Lewis and Clark expedition. They and their "Corps of Discovery" met the Blackfeet in the early 1800s; initially pleasant, their interchange eventually turned violent, which furthered the reputation of the Blackfeet as great warriors, a people with whom to be reckoned.

This violent incident occurred in the summer of 1806. Meriwether Lewis and others in the explorers' party came upon some young Blackfeet boys, who were herding horses. Apparently the meeting was initially friendly, for that evening found the boys camping with Lewis and his men—they all even competed in a footrace. Next morning, as the boys came to say good-bye, Lewis's men set upon them; nearly all were killed, except for a young boy named Wolf Calf, who would later come to be chief.

Lewis's account of this meeting differs vastly from accounts of Blackfeet tribal members whose ancestors were at the encampment. In 2003, tribal elder G.G. Kipp related his ancestor's (Wolf Calf's) version of the incident, which was recorded as part of the Blackfeet Community College Native American Scholars Program. A very similar story was also told to George Bird Grinnell (who would become known as the "Father of Glacier National Park"), who had interviewed Chief Wolf Calf in 1895. Wolf Calf's story was quite different from that of Lewis, whose journal entry said that these boys were instead "warriors" and that he and his men were set upon in the night as the "warriors" raided their camp for horses.

For a period of roughly 150 years, the Blackfeet came to be known and feared as rulers of the Great Plains. But they would eventually become statistics of "civilized progress." Unbeknownst to those who were once called the "Lords of the Plains" was that, deep below ground, underneath those plains, was another form of wealth, held by Anglo-Europeans in much greater regard than the horse. The Blackfeet people at this time were not aware that their lands contained vast riches in minerals like gold, copper, silver, oil, gas, and coal. These minerals would later attract white settlers such as mineral prospectors and cowboys in vast numbers and were a determining factor in U.S. government decisions to restrict the Blackfeet lands to a small reservation, a mere fraction of the territory they had once roamed freely, for a brief span of time, as "Lords of the Plains."

This is their story.

Culture, Religion, and Traditions

It remains a sensitive point for most Native Americans when others say that Christopher Columbus discovered America. Before his arrival, the continent was already teeming with a great variety of people, with their own social systems, diplomatic protocols, and traditions. These have been preserved as generations of people passed on their history through stories told to the young.

Like other Native Americans, the Blackfeet have a tradition of passing on their history orally. Each generation tells the stories of the earth's beginnings, as well as stories of heroes and villains, to the next generation.

The earth, and everything in, on, and surrounding it, was a source of great mystery and wonder to the Blackfeet. Especially in the olden days, when there were no scientific explanations for natural phenomena, stories were created to explain them. These accounts became part of the oral history of the Blackfeet and helped them live in harmony with the world around them. Here are a few of their stories.

HOW THE BLACKFEET CAME TO BE ON EARTH

This story is one of the more popular with modern-day Blackfeet, and it is based on a version told by an elder named Chewing Blackbones, who related it to author Ella E. Clark. The story goes like this: Old Man came from the south, and as he traveled, he made mountains, prairies, birds and other animals, forests, and favorable environments for the animals to live in. When he was finished, he rested a while; where he reclined, he made indentations in the earth, and those rolling hills are still visible today. After he rested, Old Man made grass to grow on the plains, so the animals would have something to eat. He made other plants grow, too, like carrots and turnips. Then he made the first people out of clay. They were a woman and a child. He told them his name was Napi, which means "Old Man." He showed the woman and child how to make fire and prepare food from plants and animals; he also taught them how to make and use bows and arrows, so they could hunt the animals.

As Old Man continued his travels, he made more people. He then gave them the gift of the buffalo, and from this animal the people had everything they needed for food, clothing, and shelter. Before he left his people, Old Man told them he would always care for them and would one day come back for them.

This second story has been related by elder Percy Bullchild: Long ago, the only living thing was Creator Sun. He was lonely and decided to create some companions for himself. He first made the earth from a ball of mud; from the dust of the earth, he made a snake. The snake multiplied until there were too many, and Creator Sun caused the earth to boil to kill the snakes. Only one, a female about to bear her young, survived.

Then Creator Sun made a moon as a mate for himself. After a time, the Moon gave birth to seven sons. For a time, all were happy, until one of the sons of the snake, called Snakeman, became the Moon's secret love. When Creator Sun discovered this betrayal, he and his seven sons killed Snakeman. They also killed the Moon and burned both their bodies.

Creator Sun somehow knew that the Moon would return to seek revenge, and he prepared his seven sons against this. He gave each of them a gift to use as a defense. To the youngest and oldest, he gave a bladder of water. The second youngest son was given a bird; the next son received a bladder of air. The fourth son received a stick; the fifth, a small rock; and the sixth, some magical powers.

Sure enough, a spark from the ashes—what was left of the Moon's body—flew up, and she became her old self. In a rage, the Moon hurried to her sons' camp to kill them. As they ran from the Moon, the sons used the gifts that Creator Sun had given them. The eldest son threw his water bladder at her; this became rain. The sixth son drew a line in the dirt; this became hills and steep valleys. The son with the rock threw it toward the Moon; the rock turned into high mountains. The fourth son, the one with the stick, threw it down; it became dense forests. The son with the bladder of air threw it at the Moon, and a terrible tempest blew around her. The son with the bird threw it toward the Moon, and the bird turned into the first thunder and lightning. The son with the other water bladder threw it toward her; this turned into a great flood.

All these obstacles did slow down the Moon, but she still came after them. Finally the seven sons flew up into the sky, trying to elude the Moon. Today they are known as the Big Dipper, and they are always just ahead of the Moon. Also today, all kinds of weather comes down to Earth from the sky, as the seven sons still try to slow down the Moon.

As for Creator Sun, he divided the day so part of it was dark and called this night. He did this to keep the Moon in darkness so she could not see her sons very well. He made the Moon's environment inhospitable, with no life forms on or in her, and caused her to become invisible for several days each lunar cycle (we now call this the dark of the moon). For Snakeman's betrayal, Creator Sun also punished the snakes, making them the most despised of all creatures.

Still, Creator Sun was lonely; then he remembered Earth and decided she would make a better wife. Creator Sun caused Earth to be the bearer of all life forms; but still the snakes disobeyed Creator Sun, turning into huge dinosaurs. He punished these

The Blackfeet believe Creator Sun made the buffalo as a means of providing the Plains Indians with food, shelter, tools, and a lifestyle. The buffalo became the cornerstone of Native life, as people learned to use its hide, bones, and meat to the fullest extent.

rebellious creatures with a huge flood, which destroyed the dinosaurs and made room for new animals.

After the floodwaters receded, Creator Sun took mud and made the first man; he called him Mudman. He then made Mudman sleep, took his smallest rib, and created a woman; he called her Ribwoman. Creator Sun taught these first people how to use plants and their healing powers so they could overcome illnesses; he also taught them how to use sweat baths to purify themselves and how to go on vision quests for personal spiritual growth.

HOW THE BUFFALO CAME TO THE BLACKFEET

According to one legend, Creator Sun wanted to give the Blackfeet people an animal that would not only be a cornerstone of life for them and other Plains Indians but it would also be a gift that symbolized freedom and guaranteed the continued existence of the Blackfeet. Creator Sun offered an animal that was big enough to provide a thrill and challenge in the hunt, with its hide to be used for shelter, its bones for tools, and its meat for food.

The buffalo came to the Blackfeet when Creator Sun noticed that his humans were growing thin, even though he had provided all sorts of vegetables and other plants to eat. Creator Sun took mud, made a four-legged creature from it, and blew life into its nostrils. Making the animal fall into a deep sleep as he had done with Mudman, Creator Sun took the buffalo's smallest rib and made a mate for it. When the people began to eat this "flesh-food," or meat, they began to fill out and were happy.

Creator Sun then made all the other animals, both animals and birds to be hunted and eaten and animals and birds of prey. He made both kinds to keep the numbers of animals at a manageable level, so that no single creature would become extinct. Creator Sun told the Blackfeet people that they should use all parts of any animal they killed and never waste any, and he promised that, as long as they did, they would never go hungry again.

THE O-KAN, OR MEDICINE LODGE DANCE

Although the Sun Dance was perhaps more popular with other Great Plains tribes such as the Sioux, the Blackfeet also participated in their own version, which they called the "O-kan" or Medicine Lodge Dance (but it is sometimes called the Sun Dance even among Blackfeet people). This was a lengthy ritual carried out in the late spring or early summer during a full moon. During this ceremony, Blackfeet men performed the dance as a high form of sacrifice or thanksgiving for good fortune, such as being healed from disease.

The entire tribe participated in some way in this ritual. It began with a woman of the tribe offering to sponsor the dance. She had to be highly regarded by the tribe as well as someone who believed that she had been granted a wish by the sun earlier in the year. As a sponsor, she became the Sacred Woman of the Dance and fasted for days before the ceremony.

Also just before the dance, the tribe pleaded to the sun to heal the sick and then fasted and prayed for several days. Warriors sometimes wounded themselves as a form of sacrifice, to show their gratitude for being saved from danger in the past. After this time of fasting, praying, and self-mutilation, everyone wore their best clothes and regalia and gathered together in a time of feasting and celebration.

The O-kan was also an opportunity for young warriors to exhibit their courage and their stoic ability to withstand pain, as the ritual was not for the faint of heart. They and other men who wished to be in the dance got together around the lodge of the medicine woman. They then gathered branches to build a sweat lodge in which they would purify themselves. While the participants were doing this, older warriors sat in the ceremonial lodge, telling stories of previous dances and of their own exploits long ago. When the participants were ready, specially chosen dance sponsors painted their bodies (each dancer had his own sponsor). Entering the dance lodge, the dancers wore necklaces of bone beads on a band of hide or beaded necklaces with weasel

The Many Uses for the Buffalo

For the Blackfeet, the buffalo was tangible proof that their Creator provided and cared for them. The buffalo supplied the Blackfeet with everything they needed to survive. They wasted no part of the animal; to do so would be a sign of ingratitude to their Creator.

One skill for which Blackfeet women were valued lay in dressing buffalo, which they called "Shall Be Peeled." If a woman was especially skillful at butchering a buffalo, she was held in high esteem, for through her talents she could feed others and provide them with virtually everything they needed. After the woman skinned a buffalo using a scraping tool (usually a flat stone), she would rub or abrade the hide, which made it easier to tan (or convert into leather). She used a large broad bone, such as a shoulder blade, as another tool to work hides.

Afterward, she would lay the hide on the ground and keep it flat by using stakes or she would hang it upright on a frame. She would then scrape the hide, removing hair and making the hide uniformly thin. To further soften the hide, she rubbed a mixture of liver and brains into it. How the woman prepared the hide at this stage depended on how she planned to use it. If she wanted to use the hide for robes, bedding, or winter clothing, she left hair on the hide. If she needed the hide for tipi covers, she would scrape it very smooth and cut it into shape (depending on the size of the tipi frame, at least a dozen hides would be needed to fit a tipi). To make the tipi covers waterproof, she would hold the pieces over a fire—the smoke would make the covers rain-resistant. Women helped each other in these chores, often singing special songs of thanks and joy as they worked.

The creative and clever Blackfeet woman made sure each part of the buffalo was put to more than one use. After being scraped and tanned, hides became clothing such as caps, leggings, belts, moccasins, robes, and even underwear. They also used the hide to make bags called *parfleches*, which were used to carry dried foodstuffs, like pemmican. Rawhide, or untanned hide, became blankets, shields, or even a kind of shoe for horses (and it could also be used as a kind of helmet for a horse, to protect the animal's face and head in battle). Buffalo fur was not wasted, either: It was made into pillow stuffing, saddle padding, decorated headdresses and, when braided, rope.

The Blackfeet had uses for bones and horns, too. Horns might become headdress ornaments, flasks, spoons, cups, rattles, or other useful tools. Bones became dice for games or were made into arrowheads, hide scrapers, sewing awls, or even knives.

Other body parts of the buffalo were made into utilitarian items for the Blackfeet: The elastic tendons were used to string bows and sew clothing and tipi covers. A buffalo's four-chambered stomach was used to carry water, or it was made into footwear or clothing. Buffalo dung was used as fuel for fires; even the hooves, boiled in water, were made into a sort of glue.

Since the buffalo was so important to the culture, traditions, and even survival of the Blackfeet, it was fitting that many of their religious rituals centered on the buffalo. Medicine men prayed to the buffalo as a kind of advocate between themselves and their creator; items used in rituals, like headdresses and ceremonial rattles, were made from buffalo parts. Skulls were used in almost all religious ceremonies. Medicine bundles, used for personal protection, often included some part of the buffalo. Buffalo hairballs were used in ceremonies to attract herds of buffalo to come near hunting parties.

skin hanging from them. They also wore a special cloth, which hung from their waist to their ankles; some accounts also say that the participants donned wreaths made of sage on their heads. The dance itself was extremely painful. Anyone who was able to withstand the pain and stay conscious during the dance was considered to be in superior physical shape.

The most dramatic facet of the ritual involved the dancers' piercing the flesh of their chests using a type of wooden or bone skewer; this skewer was attached by a leather thong to a pole in the center of the specially constructed dance lodge. The participants danced around the pole, attached to it by the skewers, as they sang songs and blew on whistles made from eagle bones, the sound of which they believed the Great Spirit could hear. While dancing, they focused their attention on a sacred medicine bundle tied at the top of the pole. The role of the sponsors was to encourage the dancers as they withstood the pain of the excruciating ceremony. Sometimes a young woman might give the dancers some crushed herbs to renew their strength. The dancers performed this ritual until they tore free of the skewers; this was the end of the dance. Any visions the dancers experienced during this ritual were thought to be especially meaningful and sacred. The flesh that tore from the dancers' bodies at the end of the dance was left at the base of the pole as a sacrifice to the sun.

As for the Sacred Woman of the O-kan, during the ritual she was dressed in elaborate regalia, including a special headdress, an elk-skin robe, and an antelope- and- deer-hide dress. During the dance, the Sacred Woman gave away several horses—a show of generosity was a part of the ritual. Everyone was expected to treat the Sacred Woman with high regard throughout the ceremony and thereafter.

Along with other religious customs and traditions, the O-kan was forbidden by U.S. officials once they began their attempts to "assimilate" the Blackfeet. This ban was made official in 1883, when the Bureau of Indian Affairs (BIA) came out with a publication entitled *The Code of Religious Offenses,* which forbade anyone,

The Sun Dance is a sacred tradition of various Plains Indian tribes, including the Blackfeet. Originally, young men performing this ritual were pierced in the chest with bone or wooden skewers and tied to a tall pole in the middle of the dance lodge with long, leather ropes.

including the Blackfeet, to practice such traditional rituals. Anyone who defied this law was threatened with imprisonment. Today, the dance is once again performed, with modifications (few dancers pierce their chests). The spiritual intent of the ceremony—that of thanksgiving and renewal, to realign the universe for the next year—remains at its core.

THE VISION QUEST AND PERSONAL MEDICINE

In traditional Native American culture, "medicine" is not something to be taken as a remedy for an illness. *Merriam-Webster's Collegiate Dictionary* defines this particular meaning of the word as "an object held in traditional American Indian belief to give control over natural or magical forces," but for the Blackfeet, it is a bit more than that.

To the Blackfeet and other Native Americans, "medicine" gives a person special protection; it can also be a symbol of the person's special talents. For a Blackfeet boy, the quest for his personal medicine was a part of growing up. The "vision quest" included fasting alone in the wilderness for several days. If the boy was lucky, this part of coming into manhood resulted in a vision, often of an animal. This vision would reveal to the young man his special talents or strengths. The animal itself became the young man's own personal symbol of protection; this experience was expected to help him determine his future.

Visions and medicine were not only for young men: Young women also aspired to gain their own visions. Even the older and wiser people of the tribe paid close attention to what they might learn in their visions. Similarly, dreams were given much credence as to their meanings and messages.

RELIGION IN EVERYDAY LIFE

As with many Native Americans, religion was a part of every moment in the lives of the Blackfeet people (and remains so to this day). The Blackfeet have an attitude of thanksgiving for such everyday acts as greeting the dawn, having a meal, or seeing the end of another day. This religious attitude extended even into the making of weaponry, such as bows, lances, and arrows; warriors would sing songs for divine protection as they worked.

The Blackfeet believed that all the flora and fauna—the plants and animals—surrounding them possessed powers; recognizing this helped forge a connection between all things, living and non-living. Even the wind was thought to carry messages from the Creator. This reverence for the natural world is still embedded deep within the Blackfeet people.

Although the buffalo was at the forefront of religion, the Blackfeet revered other animals as well. They held reverence for the bear, as the animal could heal itself when it was hurt and could (usually) repel other animals' attacks. The butterfly was thought to help induce sleep, and for this reason, the hair of babies was often adorned with hide cut in the insect's shape. Wolves were considered to be highly intelligent—the teachers of the animal kingdom—and so scouts for a hunting or war party often wore wolf skins as their own "medicine." Beetles were consulted before hunters went in search of buffalo herds: It was thought that their antennae would point the way, showing hunters where the great animals could be located.

In Blackfeet religion and culture, certain shapes were (and still are) held in high regard. For example, the circle is a shape with its own deep meanings. The circle represents the continuity of life, the shape of the world, the outline of the tipi frame, and even heavenly bodies like the sun and the moon. Ian Brace of the Royal Saskatchewan Museum has written that, in the Great Plains today, there are still remains of ancient circular "medicine wheels," which are stones placed in huge circles on the earth. (Their purpose and meaning depends on whom one consults.)

For spiritual consultation in pre-reservation days, every band of Blackfeet had holy people among them. These people were not just priests or shamans; they were considered prophets, with a much deeper connection to the spiritual world than other people. A shaman was often called on to predict the outcome of battles and raids, pinpoint the location of the great buffalo herds, and even find missing children. The shaman of a band was also the holder, or keeper, of a sacred bundle. As Wendy Running Crane said in an online interview: "There are several bundles sacred to the Blackfeet, including the Beaver Bundle, the Thunder Medicine Pipe Bundle, the Natoas Bundle [held by the woman who sponsored the O-kan, or Medicine Lodge Dance], Brave Dog Bundles, Horn Society Bundles, and other society bundles." She explained that the people holding the bundles were considered holy, and when consulted for help, they called on the sacred bundles for assistance. After a shaman died, or "walked the spirit road," his or her regalia was placed with the body in trees or up high. The sacred bundle was transferred to another person, usually before the shaman's death, upon which time that person would become the sacred bundle holder.

BLACKFEET SOCIETY AND ORGANIZATIONS

Author Thomas E. Mails (*Dog Soldiers, Bear Men and Buffalo Women*) states that social organizations were quite varied and flexible within each tribe. He also writes about the uniqueness of Blackfeet society, in that social ranking in the tribe was not something that was set at one's birth. Attainment of a high social rank was possible for all people as long as they followed the rules of the tribe and sought out and received many transfers (promotions).

Several other authors, such as Walter McClintock (*The Old North Trail*), have described a variety of social orders, which were different from tribe to tribe. For the Blackfeet proper, for example, he wrote about the "Doves," which was for young males; men who were going into battle—unseasoned warriors—he called "Mosquitoes." Men who had shown valor in war he called "Braves"; older men were referred to as "Bulls" and were in the Horn Society. For the women, he wrote that their society was called the "Buffalo

Social organizations within the Blackfeet included both genders and allowed individuals to promote themselves to a higher social rank. *Above,* the headgear of a warrior in the Buffalo Society.

Cow." Because of the Blackfeet people's reverence toward the buffalo, one of their most important and advanced societies was the Horn Society, in honor of buffalo bulls; the women's Buffalo Cow Society, or in Blackfeet, *Mo-to-kiks,* carried the same honor. The men's societies were, surprisingly, open to women. In an online interview, Wendy Running Crane added this little-known tidbit: "The early writers didn't acknowledge that married couples joined many societies together, so they were not really 'men's societies.'"

Each society within the tribe had its own initiation ceremonies, regalia, tribal responsibilities, and ways of interaction. Young boys were usually transferred into the Doves Society when they were prepubescent. As the boys' feats grew with their years, they rose as a group through the societies.

When reservation life became the norm instead of the exception, many societies, with their traditions and glories, passed out of the pages of history. Once on reservations, the Blackfeet came under government policies that made it illegal to practice anything resembling Indian religion—which meant the entire way of life for the Blackfeet people.

Women in Blackfeet Culture

American history books have portrayed women in Native American culture as faceless, nameless beings who carried on the menial tasks of camp life. When Europeans first came in contact with Native Americans and saw women proceeding behind the men on the trail, they mistakenly saw this as a physical statement of women's stature in Native American social structure (in reality, men went ahead of the women and children to face any dangers they might encounter). Until recently, little more than this has been written about women in Native American culture. In writing and art, the way they have been portrayed has been skewed by the mind-set of the authors and artists.

In the early 1600s, artists such as Adrien Collaert II portrayed Native American women as either one with nature or amoral, savage pagans. As time went by, artists increasingly depicted Native American women as thinner and lighter-skinned. By the late

1700s, they began to appear more like goddesses from Greek or Roman myth than as recognizable Native American women.

Author Jane Katz approached the biased portrayals of Native American women that she noted in art and writing, first posing this question in her book *Messengers of the Wind: Native American Women Tell Their Life Stories:* "Why is it that Indian and Native Alaskan women have been viewed by the larger society as passive when in fact they often play major roles within their communities and on the national scene?" In her book, she explores the misconceptions about Native American women, many of which are still evident in today's media. These misconceptions apparently stem from the worldviews of those observing the culture. In Gretchen M. Bataille and Kathleen Mullen Sands's book *American Indian Women: Telling Their Lives,* the preface states that "the positions of women in European societies, largely derived from Judaic and

Abraham Maslow's "Hierarchy of Needs" and the Blackfeet

A fascinating aspect of history is the little-known fact of how psychologist Abraham Maslow came to develop his now-famous "Hierarchy of Needs." Maslow's hierarchy was based upon the theory that, once people's basic needs were met (such as those for food and shelter), they would then address those needs that would help them develop as a person. What most people don't know is that Maslow developed this theory while living with the Blackfeet in the 1930s, which led him to observe that people grew and changed throughout their lives. Maslow's observations also reflected the fact that Blackfeet boys and girls were raised to be independent thinkers and learners and were not considered inferior to adults just because they were children.

Christian ideals of womanhood, led European men to overlook the power that Indian women could wield in their own societies."

A traditional woman of the Blackfeet people was actually held in high esteem. They did the hard work of the camp, it is true; but as Katz points out, this was taking part in "the business of survival." Women were not only caregivers; they were also healers, warriors, artists, and spiritual leaders. As Rayna Green writes in her book *Women in American Indian Society,* "Although a male-centered tribe, the Blackfoot recognized the importance of women to their society and welcomed their participation in public life." Pre-reservation Blackfeet women were given due respect for ensuring the very survival of their people. Even more than this, however, was the emphasis on balance in all things, and the Blackfeet people recognized that men and women established balance in the lives of the people and in the perpetuation of their traditions. Blackfeet culture further took note that women held equally important, but different, roles in society. Even in ceremonies, there were male and female sides of the tipi—not because women were inferior or superior, but equal and separate.

Female deities abounded in Blackfeet creation stories, emphasizing the traditional reverence the Blackfeet held toward women. In her book *The Ways of My Grandmothers,* Blackfeet author Beverly Hungry Wolf tells of Napi, the first male human, and how he was virtually helpless by himself. Napi met with the "chief of the women," who decided that they should live together in order for the men to survive.

Perhaps one reason women were seen in a negative light in the early days of contact with Europeans was because of the skewed mind-set of what author Barbara Oldershaw referred to as "amateur anthropologists." In her article "Blackfeet American Indian Women: Builders of the Tribe," she wrote that early depictions by such "experts" as artist George Catlin were based on assumptions. His opinions were influenced by the fact that he was of European descent, and he was unaware of the role that women and men

Considered to be the backbone of Blackfeet society, women took care of their own families and the overall community. Because they worked so hard, Blackfeet men respected them and treated them as equals. *Above,* Blackfeet women erect new tipis.

played in providing for tribal survival. For example, men went away from camp to hunt, fight, or raid; women, meanwhile, stayed behind, doing the day-to-day chores of maintaining camp. When the men returned from their grueling, sometimes harrowing, experiences, they would rest as the women continued their work. This led Catlin and others to falsely assume that the women were little more than slaves. Another of Catlin's contemporaries made the same false assumption. Captain Benjamin Louis E. deBonneville, an officer in the U.S. Army, lived in the Rocky Mountains from 1832 to 1835. His own limited observations led him to relate to his friend Washington Irving that "the duties of a [Blackfeet] wife . . . are little less onerous than those of a packhorse."

Catlin, deBonneville, and other early anthropologists, both "amateurs" and "experts," did not understand the importance of women in Blackfeet culture. As a consequence, they concluded that Blackfeet women were the drudges, as Oldershaw states, "at the mercy of their male counterparts." Blackfeet women today know that their female ancestors felt important and necessary to tribal survival. The Blackfeet women were the thread of continuity within their tribe, in their role in the annual O-kan Dance, in the maintenance of home life, and in their giving life to future generations. Women in Blackfeet culture were so important to their traditions, in fact, that the Blackfeet as a people have traced their lineage through the women instead of the men. This is called a matrilineal society, and it further reveals the important role women held among the Blackfeet people.

BIRTH TO OLD AGE

Before being forced to the reservation and its restrictive environment, women born or adopted into Blackfeet society enjoyed great freedom. The Blackfeet regarded babies as gifts from the Creator. When a woman was about to give birth, she usually did so away from camp. If the time came while her band was moving, the mother-to-be had her baby with the help of another woman or two and then rejoined the band when she could.

Babies were swaddled and protected in something called a cradleboard, which resembles today's backpacks, but with extra support behind the baby's head. The backboard not only supported the head, but it also protected the baby in case of a fall. The newborn was carried on his or her mother's back, although sometimes the cradleboard was leaned against a rock or a tree as the mother worked nearby.

As a baby girl grew, she learned from all women, including aunts and grandmothers, and didn't depend solely on her mother to be educated in the aspects of keeping a home, raising children, and other domestic duties like butchering animals and preparing food. If a young Blackfeet woman showed an interest beyond domestic activities, she was encouraged rather than discouraged

Designed to support the baby's head while his or her mother traveled or worked, the cradleboard allowed Blackfeet women to remain mobile and productive while caring for their children.

(many shamans, for example, were women). If she had a natural talent for riding a horse, hunting, or even making war, she was urged to cultivate these skills.

As Blackfeet girls toiled beside their female relatives, much of their history was passed down to them through stories. Thus, as they learned how to do all the tasks and duties that would be required of them when they became wives and mothers, they learned tribal history as well. They also learned the customs and rules of tribal etiquette that had been passed down by the generations of mothers before them.

By the time a girl experienced her first "moon," or menstrual cycle, she had been trained in the ways of butchering animals, preparing food, maintaining the home, moving and setting up camp, and raising children. If she also had talents such as beadwork or quillwork, she was considered to be a bride of high value.

Some accounts indicate that most Blackfeet marriages were arranged, but the bride had the final say. When a young man wanted to marry, he sent a friend or a relative with a gift of horses to the girl's family. If the girl accepted this token of engagement, she allowed the horses to mingle with her family's herd. If she rejected the offer, she either refused the horses or simply ignored them. Europeans mistakenly thought that this practice was a way of "paying" for the girl. For the Blackfeet and other Plains Indians, however, the gift of horses was a practical way to prove that a young man could provide for a prospective bride.

The engagement period itself was quite short; the wedding usually took place within a few days of the gift of horses to the bride's family's lodge. The wedding was simple, consisting in part of the bride coming into her husband's lodge with gifts and horses of her own. Some accounts indicate that the bride and groom cut their fingers and put them together, mingling their blood. A Blackfeet woman took pride in being a married person who could contribute much to her lodge and tribe. Another important aspect of married life was that, in the case of a lazy or an abusive husband, the wife could leave the marriage and take everything with her (even the lodge) that she had brought into it. Conversely, it was acceptable for a man to give his wife back to her family.

Blackfeet women were raised in a society that valued purity and modesty. Polygamy was practiced, however, and more often than not, a wife would welcome another wife as a kind of "co-worker" to help with household duties: the more hands there were, the easier the work would be. One woman working by herself, for

Women as Warriors

There are several examples from history of Blackfeet women who fought alongside their husbands. A woman born around 1870, Elk Hollering in the Water, went to war and on horse raids with her husband, Bear Chief. A Piegan warrior named Weasel Tail was married to a woman named Throwing Down. Until the birth of their first child, Throwing Down fought alongside Weasel Tail in several battles.

Perhaps the most famous Blackfeet woman warrior was known as Running Eagle, or Pitamahkan. When she was just a newlywed, her husband was killed in a battle against Crow warriors. The story goes that a brokenhearted Running Eagle prayed to the sun to allow her to avenge her husband's death. Running Eagle went on a vision quest, near what is now known as Two Medicine Lodges near East Glacier, Montana. There she fasted and prayed in a cave underneath a waterfall (the waterfall was then known as Trick Falls).

In the vision she had there, Running Eagle heard a voice that told her she would be a successful warrior, but only as long as she remained faithful to her dead husband. For years afterward, the young female warrior led raiding and warring parties successfully; she was so talented at war, she could not only keep up with her male counterparts, but she also outdid them. Just before 1860, Running Eagle was inducted into the customarily all-male Brave Dogs Society.

Shortly afterward, Running Eagle is said to have succumbed to a male warrior's attentions. The warning in her vision had been true: On the next warring venture, as Running Eagle was leading a contingency into an enemy Flathead camp, she was shot and killed. The waterfall where she had her vision is now known as Running Eagle Falls.

example, could only skin and dress perhaps 10 buffalo in a year; six women could take care of as many as 100 animals. It was customary for successive wives to be related to the first; often, a sister married her sibling's husband.

When a woman became a widow and/or older, she began to trade with others for goods and services she could no longer provide for herself. If she was adept at beadwork, for example, she might trade a pair of beaded moccasins for some meat from a larger lodge. Generosity was part and parcel of traditional Blackfeet life, and everyone cared for each other's needs.

BLACKFEET WOMEN AS HEALERS AND SPIRITUAL LEADERS

Blackfeet women were known to have practiced medicine alongside their husbands. According to Carolyn Niethammer, who wrote *Daughters of the Earth: The Lives and Legends of American Indian Women,* women played an important role in every ceremony. Blackfeet historian Wendy Running Crane added, "Additionally, only married couples could be holders of the sacred medicine bundles; when they passed it on to another holder (called a transfer), they served as advisers to the new bundle holders."

Blackfeet women enjoyed a great deal of freedom before reservation life. They were encouraged to be anything they wanted and to try to excel in virtually any area in which their talents led them. Those who became healers and spiritual leaders were always needed and revered, but never would the spirituality of Blackfeet women be more critical than when strange people appeared in their lands.

These strange people had foreign ways and habits, shaved their faces, and said they owned the land. They called themselves Americans, and the very survival of all Blackfeet people was about to be tested.

Famous Blackfeet Leaders in History

In pre-reservation times, when the Blackfeet people were hunting and living the unrestrained, semi-nomadic life on the Great Plains, their society was ruled by freedom, including freedom of choice. Each tribe had its own social mores and traditions; similarly, each tribe had its own leaders. The Blackfeet people were not governed by one chief who ruled all the bands; instead, individual chiefs oversaw the interests of each band.

Chiefs played different roles. Some were war chiefs, whose purpose was to plan strategies for battles and lead warriors in war. Peace chiefs served as mediators in disputes; they also were in charge of recording annually the major events of the tribe in something known as a "winter count," which was a hide with pictorial portrayals of these occurrences. The events might include a unique celestial phenomenon like a solar or lunar eclipse. The peace chief might paint a representation of a successful buffalo hunt or battle, a daring horse raid, a new chief being chosen, or some other remarkable occurrence. If these events were not recorded in a physical form, such as on a hide, they were set to memory and became part of the tribe's oral history. Besides being a chief, a person could become a spiritual leader or shaman; warriors who showed great valor in battles or horse raids were often chosen to lead the other warriors.

One of the responsibilities of the peace chief was to care for the winter count, a visual rendering of a major event in the tribe's history. Usually painted on buffalo hide, the winter count can depict a memorable battle or an unusual occurrence like a meteor storm.

Before the 1800s and the incursion of whites into Blackfeet territory, little was recorded regarding the men or women who were leaders among their people. Some of the later leaders had names like Running Crane, Little Plume, Bull-By-Himself, and Wolf Calf (who escaped the deadly "Corps of Discovery" attack and lived to tell it to the founder of Glacier National Park, George Bird Grinnell). Here are some brief biographies of Blackfeet leaders whose impact is still felt among the people.

RED CROW

Reportedly a great diplomat and speaker for his people, Red Crow, or Mi'k ai'stoowa, was of the Kainah Nation. His grandfather, uncle, and father all served as Kainah chiefs. In his younger days, Red Crow was a great warrior, leading battles against such enemies as the Assiniboine, Cree, Shoshone, and Crow. In 1870, as a smallpox epidemic ravaged his people, Red Crow became their leader when his father succumbed to the disease. Red Crow led his people through a difficult time in their history, when disease was rampant, bison were becoming rare, and a liquid introduced to them by the Anglo-Americans (whiskey) threatened to destroy their very existence. According to the *Alberta Online Encyclopedia*, Red Crow himself came under the influence of the spirit, and in a drunken state, killed his brother and two other Kainah tribesmen.

The whiskey trade was ended in 1874 by the North-West Mounted Police and their leader, Colonel James Macleod, whom Red Crow befriended. Because of their friendship and trust, Red Crow entered into negotiations with the Canadian government in 1877 to consider what came to be called Treaty 7, which established reserves for the tribe and promised annual payments and provisions. Red Crow was the great-grandfather of a later, modern-day leader, Clarence "Curly Bear" Wagner.

LAME BULL

Lame Bull, whose Blackfeet name was Stamiksistsekai, is probably most famous for being the first signer of the initial official treaty in

1855 between whites and the Blackfoot Confederacy (he was chosen as the head chief of the Blackfoot Confederacy when he signed this treaty, so it became known as "Lame Bull's Treaty"). He was known for his diplomacy and vision in trying to save his people. According to author Adolf Hungry Wolf, Lame Bull was killed in 1856, breaking his neck during a buffalo hunt.

MEDICINE SNAKE WOMAN

Medicine Snake Woman, whose name was Natawista, or Natoyist-Siksina, was born around 1824 in Canada, daughter to Red Deer Woman. Medicine Snake Woman's father was chief of the Blood tribe; his name was Two Sons.

Apparently Medicine Snake Woman was an adept equestrienne and a striking beauty, for both Swiss artist Rudolf Friedrich Kurz and naturalist John James Audubon described her in their writings. Audubon wrote that the young girl rode a horse every bit as well as a man; Kurz said she was "an excellent model for Venus" because of her beauty, according to the *Dictionary of Canadian Biography*.

Kurz and Audubon were not the only ones taking note of her: When she was 15, she traveled with her father to Fort Union, which was near the Montana-North Dakota border. There, she caught the eye of Major Alexander Culbertson, a trader with the American Fur Company. He was already well acquainted with her tribe, having experience in trading and diplomatic relations. Medicine Snake Woman and Culbertson married in the Blackfeet tradition in 1840.

Historians have acknowledged her contributions to the treaties that occurred after her marriage to Major Culbertson. She was present at several meetings and treaty negotiations between her people and white representatives, including the Fort Benton Council of 1853 and Lame Bull's Treaty of 1855. She became so well known that she was compared to Sacajawea as a diplomat between her own culture and the white world. Although her marriage (and a subsequent one) didn't last, her commitment to her Native roots

The Land of the Shining Mountains

Blackfeet people on both sides of the U.S.-Canadian border have long revered the 5 million-acre area they call the "Rocky Mountain Front." According to the *Welcome to Blackfeet Country!* Web site (http://www.blackfeetcountry.com), this is "the only region in the lower 48 states that is still home to all the species present at the time of the Lewis and Clark expedition." It remains part of one of the most untouched, pristine ecosystems in the United States, and there you can find such native species as bighorn sheep, elk, grizzly bear, and other large animals that still call this region of the country home. The Badger-Two Medicine part of the Rocky Mountain Front is named after two rivers in the area: Badger Creek and Two Medicine River. Accessible only by foot (as it has no roads), the area is such a wild place that it is sometimes called "America's Serengeti."

Many visitors who come to this area seem to get a "feel" for the reverence the Blackfeet hold toward it. It remains a sacred place for the Blackfeet, especially the Pikuni. The peaks that lie within the boundaries of the Rocky Mountain Front have been named to honor Blackfeet chiefs and leaders of old, with names like Running Crane, Little Plume, Curly Bear, and others. It is little wonder the state of Montana is also known as the "Land of the Shining Mountains."

did. She died in 1893 and is buried in Stand Off, Alberta. She is one of the few women with her own entry in the *Dictionary of Canadian Biography*.

HEAVY RUNNER

Born around 1830, Heavy Runner was the chief of the Piegan. On January 23, 1870, Colonel E.M. Baker attacked his band, which was peacefully camped along the Bear River. Initially called the Piegan War, this battle later became known as the Baker or Bear River Massacre. More than 200 Piegan, including Heavy Runner, were killed. The great-great-grandson of Chief Heavy Runner is Bob Burns. In a telephone interview, Burns said that his ancestor had been known among his people for his "generosity and bravery." Heavy Runner's attempts at diplomacy were well known even among whites, and he received medals and documents honoring his efforts at peace.

WHITE CALF

The last recorded head chief of the Blackfeet Nation, White Calf was known among the people as Onesta-poka. After the era of treaties was over, he was the signer of two "agreements," one in 1887 and the other in 1895, that ceded Blackfeet lands to the United States. In 1903 he was part of a delegation that went to Washington, D.C. White Calf died during this visit.

BIG LAKE

Big Lake was a head chief of the Blackfoot Confederacy in the mid-1800s and was close friends with Mountain Chief. He reportedly had an outstanding war record. Together, Mountain Chief and Big Lake led the tribe, the Blood Band of the Pikuni, for a time, according to Adolf Hungry Wolf's book, *The Blood People: A Division of the Blackfoot Confederacy: An Illustrated Interpretation of the Old Ways.*

MOUNTAIN CHIEF

Born in 1848, Mountain Chief's Blackfeet name was Ninastoko, but he was also known as Big Brave. He was present at the signing of Lame Bull's Treaty, as his father, also known as Mountain Chief, was one of its signers. His rise to prominence among his people happened when, at the age of 18, he led a war party against enemy Crow warriors. A year later, he fought hand-to-hand against the

Glacier National Park is a sacred area that belonged to the Blackfeet until hard times forced them to sell their lands to the U.S. government. The Blackfeet story of creation is believed to have taken place in Badger-Two Medicine, a location within the park.

Kootenai and their leader, Cut Nose. Although he fought tribal enemies of the Blackfeet, he was more of a diplomat when it came to dealings with whites.

Some of Mountain Chief's actions were controversial, however. In 1887, he was one of the chiefs who, faced with the starvation of their people, were forced to cede land by signing a treaty with the U.S. government. For Mountain Chief, this meant ceding the sacred area known as the Sweet Grass Hills. In 1895, again facing hardships, including smallpox and starvation, he was one of the signers of another treaty that sold land that is now Glacier National Park. (According to Wendy Running Crane, this tract includes an area known as the "Ceded Strip," which the Blackfeet today claim was not part of the boundaries of the treaty as understood by the signers. This area contains Badger-Two Medicine, a sacred place for the Blackfeet even today.)

Mountain Chief also met four U.S. presidents, assisted tourists who visited the area, and helped General Hugh L. Scott to record and preserve Plains Indian sign language for future generations. He "walked the spirit road" in 1942. (An eloquent obituary for Mountain Chief appears in Adolf Hungry Wolf's book, *The Blackfoot Papers: Volume IV, Pikunni Biographies*.)

Later days would find the Blackfeet people ever more in need of leaders who would see them through some of the most horrendous times they would ever witness—the "sad days" that would challenge their very survival.

The Nineteenth Century and "Progress"

Before the 1800s, the Native peoples living on the Great Plains, including the Blackfeet, were relatively untouched by whites. Except for fur traders and trappers, they had had little contact with Anglo-Europeans. Then the nineteenth century came, and with it, a rising threat of extinction for the Blackfeet.

The early 1800s saw the beginning of an increasing number of aggressive encounters between Anglo-Europeans and the Blackfeet. This influx of Anglo-Europeans was made worse by the tales of early trappers and explorers, who had come to an area that had been thought of as a wasteland (and had been called the "Great American Desert"). Suddenly, the Great Plains were no longer seen as a wasteland but as a huge, "uncivilized" wilderness begging for whites to come, settle, and "tame" it. When the explorers Meriwether Lewis and William Clark returned from their expedition to the Pacific Coast and arrived in St. Louis, Missouri, in 1806, they brought with them stories of an immense land teeming with game (especially the valuable beaver), just there for the taking. The findings of the Lewis and Clark expedition only served to send something akin to an engraved invitation to those who were looking for a better life, adventure, or riches. This led a large number of trappers, hoping to make their fortunes, to venture into Blackfeet country.

Trappers from British fur companies (who came from Canada) and those who were Americans quickly developed a rivalry. Trappers allied themselves with various tribes in order to have access to the land they occupied. Although the Blackfeet remained suspicious of whites because of their deadly encounter with the Lewis and Clark expedition, other tribes such as the Sioux, Crow, Nez Perce, Mandan, and Flathead befriended trappers.

During the 1810s, the Blackfeet rebuffed any attempts to open their lands to trappers. One company in particular, the Missouri Fur Company, met with resistance—on more than one occasion—as the Blackfeet defended their territory. Although the Blackfeet had pushed its trappers out of the Three Forks area in 1810, the company decided to try again in 1822. Hundreds of trappers, recruited by two men named Andrew Henry and William Ashley, came to Blackfeet country to reap the bounty of hides waiting for them. Taking river routes into the Rocky Mountains, the trappers were set upon time and again by Blackfeet warriors in 1823. More than two dozen trappers lost their lives; the rest were lucky to get away with only the losses of their guns, supplies, and furs.

The Blackfeet did eventually cooperate with fur traders, but it was more out of a sense of desperation: Intense competition between such companies as the Hudson's Bay Company and the American Fur Company led to fur-trading forts being set up in Blackfeet territory. More than a half dozen were built, including Fort Mackenzie, Fort Kipp, and Fort Edmonton. By the 1830s, most trappers left Blackfeet country for selfish reasons: The beaver was on the verge of extinction, because of overtrapping by whites.

The throngs of trappers and traders, however, were followed by settlers and cowboys, the latter of whom wanted to fence in the vast Sea of Grass. Then whites discovered a precious metal that spelled fortune for them but doom for the Blackfeet. That discovery was gold.

GOLD, GREED, AND NATIVE AMERICANS IN THEIR PATH

Once gold was discovered in Blackfeet territory in the 1850s, those whites desiring a quick and easy fortune made their way there in droves, ruthlessly seeking their share of the gold lying beneath the hills of the Great Plains and in the Rocky Mountains. The Blackfeet were at first concerned, then alarmed, and finally angered at the vast swarm of people arriving by wagon and, later, rail (this came to be known as the Great Emigration).

The lust for gold, minerals, and land that Anglo-Americans said were "just there for the taking" led to "treaties" offered to the tribes living in the Great Plains. History shows that these "treaties" served the interests of only the whites and increasingly shrank Blackfeet lands on both sides of the Canada-U.S. border.

THE TREATY OF FORT LARAMIE (1851)

The Great Emigration saw a sharp increase in the number and severity of conflicts between whites and the Blackfeet. The result was that American settlers lobbied the U.S. government for protection against Blackfeet raids (history books often fail to mention that the raids for food and supplies would probably never have happened had it not been for the whites' incursion onto Blackfeet lands and their callous disregard for Native Americans' continued survival and way of life). The lobbying efforts did not go unrewarded: In 1851, the government established the Treaty of Fort Laramie, which set the borders of the Blackfeet Nation and other tribes. The irony of the name is not lost on the Blackfeet and scholars of Native history—the "treaty" was not one in the truest sense of the word, as the Blackfeet were neither consulted nor represented in negotiations or present at its signing.

LAME BULL'S TREATY (1855)

Named after the first Blackfeet chief to sign, this treaty was the first mutually recognized document between the Blackfeet and the U.S. government. Its provisions included the U.S. government paying the Blackfeet $20,000 per year in goods and services and setting aside $15,000 annually toward the "education and Christianization" of the Blackfeet. For their part, the Blackfeet agreed to relinquish half their hunting lands, with their goal to live in "perpetual

Conflicts between white settlers and the Blackfeet happened frequently with the increase of people traveling to the West through the Great Plains. The Blackfeet grew frustrated as covered wagons, transcontinental train tracks, and telegraph poles appeared in their territory.

peace" with their new white neighbors. The treaty further allowed whites to settle on, build missions, erect telegraph systems, and lay railroad in Blackfeet territory.

Initially, relations between American whites and the Blackfeet were good, with some Blackfeet helping whites to hunt buffalo and trading hides for useful tools such as guns. After a short time, however, the Blackfeet discovered that the Americans were no longer honoring their part of the treaty. Instead of the Blackfeet people receiving food and blankets, for example, they were given rancid meat and moth-eaten wool. And the wool sometimes was tainted with the germs of a disease against which the Blackfeet had no natural immunity: smallpox. Some Blackfeet, like the Piegan, were the most frequent victims of the disease, which had begun to strike the tribe even before the treaties. The year 1837 alone saw approximately two-thirds of the Blackfeet population succumb to smallpox. Some historians believe that at this time a form of genocide was taking place, as smallpox was as effective as the bullets of soldiers when it came to diminishing the numbers of Blackfeet.

THE TRANSCONTINENTAL RAILROAD (1860s)

In addition to disease and hunger, the Blackfeet faced the problem of telegraph poles and railroad tracks marring their land. The transcontinental railroad system, made famous by the spike hammered at Promontory Point, Utah, was built between 1863 and 1869 by the Central Pacific Railroad of California and the Union Pacific Railroad. For the first time, a person could travel by rail from the east coast of the United States to the west. Although the Transcontinental Railroad did not travel through Blackfeet territory, other linking rail services did. These rail lines served to rapidly settle what had been called the Great American Desert.

The Blackfeet people did not passively accept their loss of land, the rapid disappearance of the buffalo, and the dishonesty of whites. Raids on small settlements and ranches increased throughout the

1860s, in a retaliatory protest. As tensions rose on both sides, tragedy was bound to strike the Blackfeet, and it did. This tragedy came to be known as the Baker Massacre, although many Blackfeet people refer to it as the Marias or Bear River Massacre.

"GIVING A LESSON": THE BEAR RIVER MASSACRE OF 1870

By the late 1860s, tensions were high on both sides of the struggle for land (for whites) and survival (for the Blackfeet). On the Sunday morning of January 23, 1870, the temperature was well below zero as a Piegan band of several hundred women, children, and elderly lay sleeping at their encampment beside the Bear (also known as the Marias) River. Most of them were sick with smallpox, and only a handful of able-bodied men were in the camp, as most of them had gone on a hunting expedition.

Colonel E.M. Baker led a surprise attack with his U.S. Cavalry detachment against the sickly, defenseless Piegan. Chief Heavy Runner reportedly told his people not to worry—that he would talk with Baker and his men and settle them down. Heavy Runner was known to be friendly and he had no need to be fearful—or so he thought. Walking toward Baker and his Second Cavalry, the unarmed Heavy Runner held up a medal and some official documents, items to show that he and his people were friendly and were not to be harmed. Without a word spoken, Heavy Runner was shot down. Baker's men charged through the camp, shooting everyone who moved. They ran off the horses and then piled the wounded along with the lodges in a heap and set it all on fire. By varying accounts, more than 200 Piegan are thought to have been killed in this cold-blooded massacre (only one soldier died). A handful of people—mostly children—escaped the slaughter by running and hiding nearby; many of them froze to death in the bitter cold. Survivors later told of hearing the anguished cries of their wounded loved ones as they were burned to death.

Recording Blackfeet History in Art

Over the years, quite a number of white artists helped to preserve tribal history, and perhaps no Native nation has been depicted in art and written about more than the Blackfeet. Artist Karl Bodmer, who was born in 1809 in Switzerland, accompanied the German naturalist and explorer Maximilian zu Wied-Neuweid to the United States. They traveled the American West from 1832 to 1834, with Bodmer painting images of Native peoples and "Prince Max" writing about and sketching flora and fauna.

Born in Wilkes-Barre, Pennsylvania, in 1796, George Catlin became fascinated with stories of Native Americans as a child. Catlin initially worked as a lawyer, but he followed his heart to record in art what he called America's "vanishing race," setting out from St. Louis, his base of operations, in 1830. Catlin made five trips over the next six years, visiting 50 tribes; two years later he traveled among 18 more tribes, including the Blackfeet. He painted a total of 607 depictions of Native Americans and scenes of the American West. Unfortunately, mounting debts forced him to sell what he called his "Indian Gallery" in 1852. Today, most of that gallery hangs in the Smithsonian Institution's American Art Museum's

A hearing afterward caused a general outcry of protest among Native Americans and sympathetic whites, as the story came out from the handful of Piegan survivors and the soldiers who attacked. The outrage was made worse when it was brought to light that Baker had attacked the wrong camp—he was looking for Mountain Chief's camp. Baker and other superiors nonetheless justified the attack, saying they were "giving a lesson" to the Blackfeet. Although Baker was dishonorably discharged, this mistake collection; several hundred sketches are in the American Museum of Natural History in New York City.

A lesser-known but equally talented artist was Kathryn Woodman Leighton. Born in Plainfield, New Hampshire, in 1875, she married attorney Edward Leighton and then studied art in Paris and Vienna. Early on, Leighton held a fascination for open spaces, especially the American West. When another artist, Charles Russell, told her of the beauty of Glacier National Park, she traveled there and painted many panoramic depictions of its grandeur. The Great Northern Railway purchased the entire collection of these paintings in 1926.

That same year, Leighton began to paint members of the Blackfeet tribe. They were apparently impressed with Leighton and the way she depicted them in art, for they adopted her into their tribe. Eventually, the Great Northern Railway commissioned Leighton to paint 22 paintings of Blackfeet chiefs and elders. Her paintings of Native Americans, including the Blackfeet, and her panoramic landscapes of the West can be found in art and history museums across the United States.

Artists and writers such as Bodmer, Catlin, and Leighton helped preserve a people and a time in U.S. and Canadian history that might otherwise have been lost to mainstream culture.

was wiped from his record. But it could never be wiped from the memory of the Blackfeet who survived (the massacre has since been compared to that of Wounded Knee in South Dakota, where 150 Lakota were killed in 1890).

The Blackfeet people had no choice but to continue to accept more legislation that increased their dependence on a foreign government. In the same year as the Baker Massacre, present-day Alberta, Canada, was opened to white settlement. The Canadian government established the North-West Mounted Police, known as the "Mounties," who effectively eliminated the illegal whiskey trade and won them the affection of Blackfeet chiefs, such as Red Crow.

By 1873, a new tanning process was developed that could turn buffalo hides into leather; prices skyrocketed, and hunters shot the bison by the millions. The loss of the buffalo caused the Blackfeet to depend even more on government help for food, clothing, and other necessities. In 1873, President Ulysses S. Grant issued an executive order establishing the Great Northern Reservation across much of northern Montana for the Gros Ventre, Piegan, Blood, Blackfoot, and River Crow Indians.

TREATY 7 (1877)

In 1877, Red Crow and other Blackfeet chiefs in Canada were offered a treaty (now known as Treaty 7, or T7). The treaty placed the Blackfeet on land set aside for them (called reserves). In light of all the privations their people had been enduring, the chiefs signed readily.

Moving the Blackfeet to reservations was a more peaceful and less bloody process in Canada than in the United States. This was probably because there were fewer whites at the time in Alberta, but the Canadian government did seem to be more willing to honor treaties and act respectfully toward the Blackfeet than did its southern neighbor. This treatment served to help Canada when, in 1885, several Native American tribes joined forces in an armed rebellion against the government; the Canadian Blackfeet remained loyal to Canada and refused to join in.

RESTRICTIONS IN THE UNITED STATES

South of the border, however, with their numbers depleted by disease and the buffalo nearly gone, the Blackfeet (especially the South Piegan) became totally dependent on the U.S. government for food, something they had been promised in Lame Bull's Treaty. The rations didn't always arrive; over the winter of 1883–1884, more than 600 Blackfeet died in what they came to call "Starvation Winter." The government took advantage of their resulting vulnerability and, in 1887, took land away from the Blackfeet reservation in Montana. From a reservation that once took in almost two-thirds of eastern Montana, the Blackfeet found themselves on a much smaller tract of land in the northwest corner of Montana's Great Plains. The Blackfeet reservation lands were further

The U.S. government hoped to eliminate Native American culture and assimilate people like the Blackfeet into mainstream society. The Blackfeet were restricted from leaving the reservation and were forbidden to speak tribal language or practice their traditional religion.

restricted in 1895, leaving them entirely within strict boundaries and dependent upon a government alien to them.

While the U.S. government was reducing the Blackfeet reservation in 1887, it was also instituting policies affecting other Native Americans. That year, Congress enacted the General Allotment Act, or Dawes Act, which allotted tracts of land to individual Indians; any reservation lands not allocated were open to be sold to the public. At the time, the Dawes Act did not impact the Blackfeet, but they would face Allotment starting in 1907.

The Blackfeet did feel the brunt of other government policies, though, as the United States sought to force Native Americans to become part of Anglo-American culture—the new program was "assimilation"—and took away the freedoms that mainstream Americans enjoyed as their basic rights. These policies made it illegal for Native Americans, including the Blackfeet, to practice their traditional religion, speak their tribal language, and continue to learn their history through their tribal elders as was their custom. The Medicine Lodge, or O-kan Dance, was expressly forbidden. The children especially were the targets of "Assimilation."

BOARDING SCHOOL, RELIGION, AND ASSIMILATION

Imagine being a young child or teenager, living with your family and extended family. Imagine your home life may not have all the comfortable amenities as many homes, but it's still your home, a place for your family to gather and be themselves. Now imagine being forcibly removed from that home. You're forced to live away from your family, your hair is cut off, you're not allowed to sing songs your family taught you, and you're forbidden from speaking your own language—if you do, you're beaten.

This experience was shared by generations of Blackfeet children during Assimilation days. The U.S. government believed that the main way it could prevent Native American traditions and culture from being passed on was to remove the children from their homes and teach them what it wanted them to know. The children were sent to be educated in government-established boarding schools on and off the reservation. Suddenly, Blackfeet children on both sides of the border were alienated from their own people. They were taught to view their culture and traditions as shameful and even akin to witchcraft, and were told that they must live like mainstream Americans.

Catholic Jesuit missionaries, called "Black Robes" by the Blackfeet, became a major assimilating force on the reservations. Besides teaching their own religion to the Blackfeet, the missionaries showed them how to farm and raise cattle. They did achieve some positive results, however, in preserving Blackfeet culture: The missionaries learned the Blackfeet language and translated religious texts into that language. They also helped preserve peace between white settlers and the Blackfeet, serving as mediators. Eventually other religions established missions and schools on the reservations, lessening the influence of the Black Robes.

The grim years the Blackfeet people had survived led to new issues that lay ahead. The early to mid-twentieth century would bring even more challenges to the Blackfeet people to preserve their culture and history while somehow managing to survive in the new environment in which they found themselves.

The Blackfeet People in the Early to Mid-Twentieth Century

As if it wasn't enough for the Blackfeet to suffer being forced onto reservations (called reserves in Canada), lose their traditional ways of living and religious ceremonies, and lose their children to boarding schools and the "Assimilation" policies of the U.S. government, they were bound to endure equally great challenges in the early to mid-twentieth century. The beginning of the 1900s dawned with hopes growing dim.

In Canada in the early 1900s, the Department of Indian Affairs decided that the Blackfeet would become more "civilized" if they lived in huts or cabins instead of tipis. The result was that many people wound up living in tiny, dark dwellings that were little more than hovels and nurtured disease. Tuberculosis and an eye disease called trachoma grew rampant in this new alien lifestyle, and the Blackfeet population was ravaged on both sides of the border. (Trachoma is a bacterial infection of the eye and is often found among people living in poverty and crowded, unhygienic conditions. Untreated, trachoma can lead to blindness.) The North Piegan in Canada lost 50 percent of their population from 1888 to 1909. The South Piegan on the U.S. side also fared poorly, with most of their people suffering from tuberculosis or trachoma.

Between the 1880s and 1907, both governments attempted various programs that were meant to "civilize" their Blackfeet charges (the Blackfeet saw their nation as a sovereign one, but neither Canada nor the United States recognized this). Some programs tried to force the Blackfeet into a totally agrarian way of life; others tried to encourage ranching. All of the programs were seriously underfunded—or the people in charge were the ones who usually benefited. Often, the Blackfeet who were supposed to "benefit" from these programs wound up nearly starving to death. Only by the 1900s did the Kainah and South Piegan realize a little success with raising cattle. Struggling as they were, the Blackfeet people as a whole could at least call the land they stood on theirs—that is, until the Blackfeet Allotment Act was forced upon them.

THE BLACKFEET ALLOTMENT ACT (1907)

When the U.S. Congress passed this act, it dealt a severe blow to the South Piegan. Native American culture views land in a communal way—no one "owns" land, and upon first hearing a white person make claim to land, many Native people would have laughed at the joke. But this was not a joke, and the South Piegan weren't laughing. The Blackfeet Allotment Act was passed without the consent of the South Piegan; it broke up their tribal reservation into smaller units of land that were then assigned, or allotted, to individuals. Although this act violated an agreement made in 1895, in which the U.S. government vowed never to take this very action, it happened anyway. The South Piegan were further alarmed when the resulting "surplus" lands—some 800,000 acres—were scheduled to be opened to white settlement.

The allotment act was an abysmal failure for the Blackfeet people, as the allotted lands were too small to ranch or too poor or impractical to farm. After this, even more South Piegan were swindled out of their lands, as allotments could be sold to non-Indians. To make the situation worse, the allotments were taxed; nonpayment resulted in seizure of the land by the state and federal government, which then sold it to local white merchants, ranchers, and others who wanted Blackfeet lands for themselves.

North of the U.S. border, the Blackfeet fared little better. In Canada, Blackfeet could not sell their allotments to non-Blackfeet, but they were pressured by Canadian officials to sell their allotments in exchange for extra rations. Starvation and economic necessity saw the North Piegan selling a fourth of their lands, and the Siksika half of their lands from 1900 to 1920.

Through all these hardships, one event helped bring about positive change for the Blackfeet on both sides of the border. That event was World War I.

NATIVE AMERICANS GAIN CITIZENSHIP (1924)

After World War I broke out, Blackfeet in Canada and the United States tried to enlist to serve their countries, to fulfill their traditional roles as warriors. They were discouraged by officials who wanted to keep the Blackfeet on their reservation lands. As the war escalated, however, Blackfeet in both countries were allowed to join the military; they served with honor in Europe. Other Blackfeet who remained at home were encouraged to farm on a more extensive level; often, these efforts went unrewarded. The Kainah, for example, who had achieved some success with cattle farming, were sabotaged by agents on their reserve. These agents used this time to line their own pockets, since they were given free use of Blackfeet resources due to wartime directives to increase agricultural output. Instead of using their authority to help the Kainah increase the number and health of their cattle, the agents neglected them and most of the herd died off. Some Kainah saw this as an attempt to break them financially and force them to give up more of their lands, as agents became rich. There were, however, positive

Canadian and U.S. Blackfeet who fought in World War I were awarded U.S. citizenship. Later, thousands of Blackfeet men and members from other Native American groups would serve in World War II (*above*).

results of World War I, one of which was the granting of citizenship to all Native Americans in the United States.

In 1924, Native Americans, including the Blackfeet, were awarded U.S. citizenship (Canada granted citizenship to its indigenous people in the 1960s). The law was enacted to reward Native

Americans for their part in helping to win World War I. While being recognized as American citizens was certainly a help to the Blackfeet and other Native Americans, it did not protect them from the poverty that largely resulted from the Blackfeet Allotment Act. To aid in this problem, the U.S. Congress passed the Indian Reorganization Act (IRA) in 1934.

THE INDIAN REORGANIZATION ACT OF 1934

The IRA put an end to doling out allotments to individual Native Americans. It also served to protect tribal boundaries and allowed all Native people to organize sovereign tribal governments (these governments, however, had to be patterned after white government rather than be based on traditional tribal ways). Additionally, the IRA provided more funds for institutions like schools and financial aid in the way of credit programs. Taking advantage of the IRA, the Blackfeet Tribal Business Council (BTBC), which formed in 1915, coordinated the adoption of a tribal constitution in 1935, and a charter of incorporation in 1936. That year, Native Americans were granted Social Security benefits, and in 1937 a hospital was built on the Blackfeet Reservation. Many Blackfeet saw this time as an opportunity to have more of a say in their lives. The 1930s had planted a seed; it was time for that seed to take root and grow.

THE "NEW BUFFALO": OIL

Emboldened with new constitutional powers and an IRA charter of incorporation, Blackfeet leaders turned toward what was to become their "new buffalo," or source of sustenance. Their land, they found, was rich in oil, and they could use this resource to help their people and to further their claims to sovereignty. The BTBC began to lease reservation land to oil companies that wished to do exploratory drilling. With these funds as well as income from logging and farming, the Blackfeet began to see some economic improvement. This period of small successes, however, brought with it new challenges: Who was to benefit from these sources of income? Also, who would be making the decisions for the people?

In the 1930s (and even before then), a distinction began to form between full-blooded Blackfeet (called "full-bloods") and mixed-blooded ones (called "half-bloods"). As the number of half-bloods grew, so did their domination of the reservation's economy. When the half-bloods pushed for legislation to sell more Blackfeet lands to further their own interests in the cattle industry, they were violently opposed by the full-bloods, who were still resentful over the loss of the Sweet Grass Hills and the Glacier lands (sold in earlier legislative moves). The BTBC, whose members were predominantly half-bloods, found itself in opposition to the full-blood-dominated Piegan Farming and Livestock Association (PFLA) as a result.

In the 1920s and 1930s, this intra-ethnic conflict was lessened somewhat as leaders of both sides worked together to grow the Blackfeet tribe's oil and grazing business. Mountain Chief was the most vocal person in speaking for tribal unity, at one point wrapping himself in an American flag and telling the people gathered, "We are all one blood." In the early 1930s, however, and even into the mid-1940s, resentment remained between the full-bloods and the half-bloods. The tradition and spirit of the "giveaway," in which those who had more gave to those who had less, was still held dear by the full-bloods, while the half-bloods were embracing modern-day capitalism. As time went by, the full-bloods—who were often the elders, with fewer resources and poorer health—found themselves slipping economically.

The BTBC responded to the needs of these people by giving them funds for medical treatment and loans, among other things. Still dissatisfied, the full-bloods sent letters of complaint to the Bureau of Indian Affairs in 1942. Among their complaints was opposition to the Indian Reorganization Act, which they said they wanted to do away with completely. In 1945 the BTBC responded with a constitutional convention, during which they explained the parameters of the constitution and their goals for the people.

Blackfeet Warriors (World War II and the Korean War)

In *Army History: The Professional Bulletin of Army History*, Thomas Morgan wrote of the contributions of the "first citizens" of the United States—those of the Native Americans. During World War II, Morgan said, more than 44,000 Native Americans saw military service, serving on all fronts in the conflict and receiving numerous awards for their valor, including Purple Hearts and Congressional Medals of Honor. So eager were they to serve their country as warriors that in 1942, 99 percent of all eligible male Native Americans had registered for the draft. Many Native warriors waited in line for hours to sign their draft cards, but some Blackfeet (Morgan wrote) mocked the need for a conscription bill at all, asking when had it ever been necessary for an able-bodied Blackfeet warrior to draw lots to fight?

Blackfeet women served in the military and at home by tending "victory gardens" and working in factories. Besides using human resources, the war effort tapped into Native Americans' mineral resources as well: During World War II, the government drilled wells all over the reservation, and while the Blackfeet had received remuneration for their oil before this time, they received little compensation for oil taken during this era.

World War II and the Korean War (the veterans serving in that conflict totaled 10 percent of the Blackfeet population, according to Keith Heavy Runner, the tribe's director of veterans affairs) served to create an environment for whites and Native Americans to work together for a common cause—protecting their country. Serving side by side in the military also helped break down racial barriers between the two groups, which would help set the stage for the civil rights movement.

They also held a vote to determine what blood quantum would be required for people to receive money for oil leases, a decision that especially pleased the full-bloods. ("Blood quantum" describes an individual's degree of ancestry.)

Following the start of World War II, men and women from various Native American groups, including Blackfeet, served in the armed forces. Three Marine Corps women reservists are shown above in this 1943 photograph. *Left to right*: Minnie Spotted Wolf, Celia Mix, and Viola Eastman. A member of the Blackfeet, Minnie Spotted Wolf was the first Native American woman to enlist in the U.S. Marine Corps.

NATIONAL CONGRESS OF
AMERICAN INDIANS (1944)

The National Congress of American Indians (NCAI) was founded by Native Americans in Washington, D.C. (and a Blackfeet, Chief Earl Old Person of the South Piegan, served as president of the NCAI for a term). According to the group's Web site, its mission today is to "inform the public and federal government on tribal self-government, treaty rights, and a broad range of federal policy issues affecting tribal governments." The founding of the NCAI was one of the first major steps toward self-determination for Native Americans in the modern age. The 1940s was perhaps the beginning of a realization among Native Americans that the tide might be turning in their favor, and the hope that had almost died was rekindled in the least expected way: with World War II and the Korean War.

AN UNEXPECTED TWIST: TERMINATION

During the 1940s, the U.S. Congress developed a plan to end the federal government's relationship with Native American tribes. They called this plan "Termination" and said it would save the federal government untold millions if it turned over the tribes' affairs to each tribe's control. The government would no longer be responsible for health care and education, and members of terminated tribes would pay taxes on their land, income, and housing. For some Native Americans, this sounded like a good deal.

Some tribes that agreed to Termination found themselves in much worse shape than before. Their economies were shattered, and they lost much of their reservation lands (some of which were later returned to them). For the Blackfeet people, much debate was given to the idea of Termination. Although the federal government wanted to terminate the Blackfeet, thereby eradicating their sovereign status, Blackfeet leaders fought to preserve their sovereignty and rights as laid out by treaties. The IRA, with its democratic votes and decision making, had politicized the Blackfeet, and they dealt successfully with federal coercion, sidestepping the attempt at Termination and keeping the rights that had been promised to them in treaties.

The Blackfeet People in the Mid-to Late Twentieth Century

As the world moved into the 1950s and beyond, the term *civil rights* was increasingly in the forefront of the news. Today, when people think of the civil rights movement, most only recall the struggles of African Americans. But it was a time for Native voices demanding to be heard—and heeded—as indigenous groups like the Blackfeet came to regard constitutional rights as those for everyone.

Martin Luther King Jr.'s famous "I Have a Dream" speech resonated in the imaginations of Native people everywhere, as they began to protest government mistreatment in the 1960s. Later, the phrase "Red Power" came into being, as the civil rights movement brought with it hope for all Native Americans. Maybe, just maybe, civil rights meant justice, rather than "just us," and Native peoples, including the Blackfeet, might begin to realize a resurgence of pride and assertiveness in their culture, traditions, and rights as American citizens. A movement was afoot—it was called the American Indian Movement, or AIM. Founded in 1968, AIM advocated activism and decided to take over federal property to increase public awareness of the plight of all indigenous peoples.

THE TAKING OF ALCATRAZ

Many people who tour the old prison remains on Alcatraz Island in San Francisco Bay are surprised when they are reminded of what else this island once stood for: Native American rights. Alcatraz was made a symbol of indigenous peoples' freedom on September 10, 1969, when Native American protesters, including Blackfeet, took control of it. Originally built in 1934 on a 22-acre island, the federal prison at Alcatraz was shut down in 1963, as it had fallen into disrepair. Now, Alcatraz became an emblem for Native Americans and their protests against a government that had broken virtually every treaty it had ever made with them. As an increasing number of Native Americans arrived on the island, they took up the cry of "Alcatraz is not an island, sovereignty is the goal."

Although the Coast Guard and other officials tried to prevent people from arriving on Alcatraz, San Francisco area residents helped them get to the former island prison. The occupation caught the media's attention, domestically and internationally, and helped bring scrutiny to the unfair and cruel treatment of all indigenous peoples.

Native American activists felt it was more than time for such a protest to happen, with unemployment on reservations at 75 percent and suicide rates 10 times the national average. Depression and alcoholism were also rampant, spread like a virus among Native peoples. Native Americans were also protesting a program the U.S. government had implemented called "Relocation," which was supposedly put in place to offer job training. One stipulation of the program was that Native people were obliged to leave their reservations to get the training, often having to go to cities far from their homes and families. The resulting isolation caused many to drop out of the program, which ran contrary to their cultural

In 1969, members of the Blackfeet joined Indian activists who seized control of Alcatraz Island in San Francisco Bay. The group hoped to bring attention to the terrible living conditions on reservations and the unfulfilled treaty promises made by the federal government.

values. Some did stay and receive the training, but support for them was dropped as soon as they became employed. Relocation was part of the Termination program, but it left indigenous people vulnerable and barely surviving, alone in strange and often dangerous parts of cities.

The Public Broadcasting System aired programs on Relocation and other issues impacting Native Americans, as the occupation of Alcatraz grew from a handful of AIM members to more than 100 Native people living on the island. (Vicky Santana, a Blackfeet activist and attorney, was one of the voices of protest there. Santana "walked the spirit road" in 2009.) When the occupation ended on June 11, 1971, the protesters left with a new sense of identity as people who had rights and were going to claim those rights.

AIM members later staged similar acts in an attempt to force the U.S. government to make right the many wrongs it had committed against the First Americans. They raided the offices of the Bureau of Indian Affairs and the *Mayflower II,* a replica ship of the original *Mayflower,* when it was anchored in Plymouth Harbor, Massachusetts. In 1973, to protest conditions on the Pine Ridge Lakota Sioux reservation in South Dakota, AIM members occupied the massacre site known as Wounded Knee. They remained on the site for more than 70 days, and two of their members were killed during the standoff.

AIM has since reorganized and still fights for indigenous peoples' rights, but these days it uses more legal forms of protests. The organization had set the stage for other Native Americans to use legal means to press for their rights; it was during this time that the Native American Rights Fund (NARF) was founded.

NATIVE AMERICAN RIGHTS FUND (1970)

In the 1960s the U.S. government began new programs meant to address some of the social problems facing the country. The Office of Economic Opportunity started a program to offer legal

Oscar Bear Runner, a member of the American Indian Movement (AIM), stands guard at Wounded Knee during AIM's protest occupation in 1973. The subsequent standoff between AIM and the federal government lasted 71 days. Several people were killed.

representation to those who couldn't afford it (this was part of President Lyndon B. Johnson's "War on Poverty"). Some representatives near reservations or communities with large Indian populations discovered that Native American legal problems were unique and were controlled by what was referred to as "Indian Law," which was affected by previous court decisions, old treaties, government rulings, and myriad regulations. Very few lawyers were therefore willing (or probably able) to represent Indians as a result; the few who did worked on a basis in which they were sure to get remuneration as a result. Since few cases were taken on a contingency basis, many legal issues never saw the inside of a courtroom. At this time, the Ford Foundation met with California Indian Legal Services (CILS) to consider creating a program that would serve the legal needs of the country's Native American population. In 1970, the Ford Foundation gave CILS a planning grant, and the Native American Rights Fund was founded.

Lawyers from NARF traveled across the country to discover exactly what were the legal issues Native American communities faced. NARF also settled on where to put its offices, and in 1971 moved to Boulder, Colorado. Eleven Native people were chosen to be on a steering committee to govern NARF's activities. These people were selected based on their tribal affiliation (which would ensure a more comprehensive representation) as well as their involvement in and knowledge of Native American issues. In 1971, NARF also opened an office in Washington, D.C., to assist in its interactions with Congress and federal agencies. In 1972, the Carnegie Corporation of New York gave NARF funding to establish the National Indian Law Library, which is a national repository for Indian legal materials and resources. In 1984, NARF set up another office in Anchorage, Alaska, to help Alaska Natives with issues of tribal sovereignty, mineral rights, and subsistence hunting and fishing rights.

As far as the Blackfeet people go, NARF and its attorneys have been instrumental in pursuing the case *Cobell v. Salazar*. Without NARF's existence, the case for the rights of Blackfeet people would have long been settled to their detriment.

The Native American Rights Fund (NARF) was established to help impoverished indigenous communities acquire representation for legal matters. John E. Echohawk cofounded NARF in 1971 and created the National Indian Law Library in 1972.

THE INDIAN SELF-DETERMINATION AND EDUCATION ASSISTANCE ACT

Signed into law in 1975, this act put an end to the policy of Termination and acknowledged the autonomy of tribes (for them to determine, on their own, their collective future). Despite all this legislative progress, there remained another pressing need for all Native American people—preservation and reclamation of their ancestors' remains. Imagine if your grandmothers' or grandfathers' graves were broken into, and items were taken from their caskets or even from their bodies. White Americans would be outraged at such occurrences, but for Native Americans, this sacrilege had been going on for hundreds of years. It was time for the government to act to prevent future injustices.

NATIVE AMERICAN GRAVES PROTECTION AND REPATRIATION ACT

In 1990, President George H.W. Bush signed into law the bill known as the Native American Graves Protection and Repatriation Act, or NAGPRA. This act authorized sovereign tribes, including the Blackfeet, to have their ancestors' remains and artifacts repatriated, or returned, to their people. Because of NAGPRA, many Blackfeet who are current holders of sacred medicine bundles received them through the intervention of people assigned to protect sovereign interests and ancestral remains and artifacts. (In other words, these bundles had been held as "artifacts" by museums, and because of NAGPRA, those museums had to return the items to the Blackfeet). While NAGPRA has been viewed as mostly positive for the Blackfeet people, the law has not been without controversy. Museums around the country, even around the world, have not easily given up claims to artifacts they view as their own possessions, and repatriation is often an emotion-laden event.

HOUSING AFTER THE GREAT FLOOD

The living conditions offered Blackfeet people were substandard at best. In June 1964, a flood changed the lives of the Blackfeet people forever. The rising waters of the Two Medicine River destroyed a dam, which in turn destroyed many homes. The flood killed 30 people, including a grandmother and five children in one family, and made many others homeless. Before the flood, people had

A "Viet Cong at Wounded Knee"

Woody Kipp is a Vietnam War veteran, Blackfeet citizen, and former member of the American Indian Movement. Blackfeet veterans affairs director Keith Heavy Runner has reported that 15 percent of the able-bodied Blackfeet population served in the Vietnam War.

In his autobiography *Viet Cong at Wounded Knee: The Trail of a Blackfeet Activist*, Kipp recalled the amazement he felt when, as a "foot soldier" for AIM, military flares and search-lights of armored vehicles surrounded him during the stand-off at Wounded Knee. It was then, he realized, that he had become the enemy of the country he had just defended with his own life in Vietnam. It was then, he wrote, that he was akin to the Viet Cong—on his own soil. Kipp received the Writer of the Year Award from the Word Craft Circle of Native Writers and Storytellers for his work.

lived on their allotments of land in their substandard houses; after the flood, many close-knit families were scattered and settled into nearby towns like Heart Butte and Browning, Montana. Although their families were not close geographically, the quality of their homes improved: At first the people lived in so-called flood homes; then in the 1990s these were replaced with improved Housing and Urban Development (HUD) home sites. Finally, HUD allowed the Blackfeet Housing Authority to construct homes on the former allotted lands, and some families were able to return to where they used to live. Even with all these issues and more, the twentieth century closed with a renewed sense of hope and purpose for the people of the Blackfoot Confederacy.

Blackfeet
in the Twenty-first
Century

The people of the Blackfoot Confederacy are beginning to thrive in the modern world, but challenges remain. One challenge appears to be that the U.S. government will never admit that there was ever a genocide on this continent, and until this happens, many Blackfeet people feel that true healing can never occur. Native American activist and author Winona LaDuke, for example, said this in a 1993 lecture at Yale University: "It was a holocaust of unparalleled proportions. . . . Fifty million indigenous people in the Western Hemisphere perished in a sixty-year period." LaDuke also referred to the years of oppression of indigenous peoples as "the largest holocaust in world history." The term *holocaust* when applied to the Native American experience is not original; it has been echoed by others as well. For example, in Paul Rosier's article "They Are Ancestral Homelands: Race, Place, and Politics in Cold War Native America, 1945–1961," he noted that, as a part of Soviet Cold War propaganda, Moscow radio broadcasts declared American Indians to be "the most underprivileged people in the United States" and referred to reservations as "huge concentration camps."

ACHIEVEMENTS OF INDIVIDUAL BLACKFEET

Thanks to many people on both sides of the Canadian-U.S. border, however, this tragic period of history is being overtaken by a brighter day, as the Blackfeet continue to be a positive force in the future of the modern world. Although a few of them have recently "walked the spirit road," here are some brief biographies of modern-day Blackfeet people who have made a difference.

Elouise Pepion Cobell The great-granddaughter of Mountain Chief, Cobell has been at the forefront as an advocate for the Blackfeet and other indigenous people. She has served as chair of the Blackfeet National Bank, co-chair of the Native American Bank (and was also one of its founders), trustee of the National Museum of the American Indian, and treasurer of the Blackfeet Nation. She is perhaps best known for her class-action lawsuit, now known as *Cobell v. Salazar,* which has charged the U.S. government with trust mismanagement. For her courage and activism, she has received many awards and honors, among them the John D. and Catherine T. MacArthur Foundation "Genius Grant" (in 1997).

Beverly Hungry Wolf Born in 1950 to Edward and Ruth Little Bear, she is of the Blood tribe in Alberta, Canada. Beverly was raised on the Blood reserve and lived much like a traditional tribal person, as many of her relatives were proud of their heritage. It was only when she went to boarding school on the reserve that she learned to speak English and learned modern ways. After college, she became a teacher at St. Mary's Indian School in Alberta. Around this time, she decided to help preserve the old ways of her

Following in the footsteps of her great-grandfather Mountain Chief, Elouise Pepion Cobell has dedicated her life to helping the Blackfeet and other Native American groups. *Above,* Cobell greets Secretary of the Interior Ken Salazar following the December 2010 announcement that the U.S. government would award a $3.4 billion settlement to Native Americans for trust mismanagement.

people. She met Adolph, a writer of German descent who was so enamored with the ways of her tribe that he wanted to be adopted into it. He was given the last name "Hungry Wolf" after this happened; the couple married in 1971. They now have five children and live immersed in the traditional culture of her people in the British Columbian Rockies. She has written at least seven books, including *The Ways of My Grandmothers.* Adolf Hungry Wolf has also written about his adopted people, in an effort to preserve their culture. After more than four decades of working with and listening to tribal elders as well as collecting stories, anecdotes, and photographs of the Blackfeet people, he created an awe-inspiring four-volume set of books entitled *The Blackfoot Papers*.

Earl Old Person Having served as Blackfeet tribal chairman from 1950 to 1988 and again from 1990 to 1998, Earl Old Person has been very committed to the advancement of his people. He has been a major voice in support of Blackfeet education, and under his leadership the tribe built Blackfeet Community College in Browning, Montana. Old Person also remains a staunch advocate for the development of opportunities for the Blackfeet people, and he served one term as president of the National Congress of American Indians. In 1998, the American Civil Liberties Union of Montana presented him with its highest honor—the Jeannette Rankin Civil Liberties Award. The Institute for Tribal Government, which was established in part to provide training for elected tribal leaders,

Earl Old Person, a longtime Blackfeet leader, served as tribal chairman for more than four decades. As a former member of the American Indian Movement, Old Person is known for protecting Native American interests at a national and local level.

interviewed Old Person during its "Great Tribal Leaders" Project. He was awarded an honorary doctorate from The University of Montana as well. In 2010 Old Person wrote a retirement address to the Blackfeet Nation; he is now involved in archiving tribal records and artifacts, and continues to pass on oral histories and songs of the Pikuni. He has two Blackfeet names: "Changing Home" and "Cold Wind." He has given Indian names to high-ranking people such as University of Montana president George M. Dennison, who was called "Fast Buffalo Horse," which was also the name of Old Person's father.

Clarence "Curly Bear" Wagner Best known for his activism in the realm of repatriation of ancestral remains, Wagner "walked the spirit road" in 2009 at the age of 64. A former member of the American Indian Movement, he remained very much the activist in his later years, helping to ensure passage of the Native American Graves Protection and Repatriation Act in 1990. Wagner was also an advocate for nurturing better understanding between cultures; in this role, he helped establish the interpretive program at Glacier National Park entitled "Native America Speaks." He was also featured in an American Public Television documentary, *A Blackfeet Encounter,* which told the Blackfeet side of the deadly meeting with members of the Lewis and Clark expedition and was presented by Native American Public Television in 2006.

Joe Crow Shoe He was a revered North Piegan elder who, until his passing, was instrumental in the establishment of an interpretive center, now known as Head-Smashed-In Buffalo Jump (named for a nearby site where Blackfeet ancestors stampeded buffalo over a cliff). The center, located east of the Porcupine Mountains in Alberta, serves as a place where people are educated about Blackfeet tradition, culture, and wisdom. His son, Dr. Reg Crow Shoe, continues the tradition of passing on Blackfeet culture and pride; among other things, he is the narrator of an online, interactive teaching and learning experience entitled "Four Directions Teachings," which explains the Blackfeet worldview and many other aspects of their culture.

Steve Reevis Reevis, whose Blackfeet name is Yellow Wolf, went with his brother to watch him audition for a role as a stunt double in a movie, *War Party,* in the late 1980s. Reevis decided to try out and was hired to be the stunt double for actor Billy Wirth. Since then he has appeared in such movies as *Crazy Horse* (made for TV in 1996), *Fargo* (1996), *Last of the Dogmen* (1995), *Geronimo: An American Legend* (1993), *Dances with Wolves* (1990), and the 2005 version of *The Longest Yard,* with Burt Reynolds and Adam Sandler.

Alvin William "Dutch" Lunak Born in 1952, Lunak also appeared as a stuntman in *Dances with Wolves.* Lunak has also been in such movies as *The Last of the Mohicans* (1992), *Geronimo: An American Legend* (1993), *The Jungle Book* (1994), and *Hidalgo* (2004).

James Welch Born in 1940, Welch attended schools on the Blackfeet and Fort Belknap reservations. He received his bachelor of arts degree from The University of Montana, where he discovered his talent for writing. His works include *Winter in the Blood* (1974), *Killing Custer: The Battle of Little Bighorn and the Fate of the Plains Indians* (1994), and *Fools Crow* (1986), the latter of which was a work of historical fiction about the Bear River Massacre of 1870. While his works have been hailed for their lyrical prose, they have also been called "unrelievedly depressing." *Fools Crow* was reviewed as being on-par with books like *Lonesome Dove* and *House Made of Dawn.* Welch "walked the spirit road" in 2003.

Other notable people include Shannon Augare, who is active in politics and has served as a state representative in Montana; and artists King Kuka, Terrance Guardipee, and Lyle Omeasoo. According to Wendy Running Crane, the image on the U.S. "buffalo nickel" is Two Guns White Calf, a chief who lived from 1872 to 1934. In an e-mail interview, she added, "Our firefighters are renowned for their skill and bravery. Our basketball athletes are famous in the state of Montana. . . . Our cross country athletes have won more consecutive state titles than any other high school in the nation." She also noted the high rate of Blackfeet people involved in government in Montana and in the city of Browning: the sheriff is Blackfeet, the mayor (Lockley J. Bremner, Wendy Running Crane's brother) is Blackfeet, and virtually 100 percent of the city council (and Glacier County elected positions) are of tribal origin.

WHERE THE BLACKFEET ARE

The people of the Blackfoot Confederacy live on three reserves in Alberta, Canada, and a 1.5 million-acre reservation centered in Browning, Montana (the capital of the Blackfoot Confederacy), although many Blackfeet are scattered in cities around North America and throughout the world. In Canada, the Kainah Nation Reserve is near Cardston; the Siksika, near Calgary; and the Pikanni (or Pikuni) near Pincher Creek. The people in the Montana reservation are known as the Amskapi Pikuni.

Census figures from 1990 indicate that the total population of all bands on the reservations was approximately 32,000, but according to the 2000 U.S. Census figures, more than 85,000 people in the country claimed to be of Blackfeet descent. The Amskapi Pikuni have nearly 17,000 enrolled tribal members, of which more than half live on the Montana reservation; the rest live in Alberta, Canada. Blood quantum determines whether one can enroll in any tribe of the Blackfoot Confederacy—for the Amskapi Pikuni, the minimum requirement for tribal enrollment is currently set at one-quarter, or 25 percent.

THE TRIBAL SUPREME COURT PROJECT

The issues of sovereignty and tribal jurisdiction continue to be at the forefront of Blackfeet concerns. As the new millennium dawned on the world, Native Americans, including the Blackfeet, saw an alarming erosion of their sovereignty, or self-governance. Judges were making decisions that threatened the sovereignty of all indigenous tribes. These judges lacked a basic understanding of the history of federal Indian law and policies. One noted Indian law scholar, David Getches, stated that indigenous tribes had lost approximately 80 percent of all cases that were brought before the U.S. Supreme Court over the past two decades. Getches wrote several articles protesting this injustice. One in particular, entitled "Beyond Indian Law: The Rehnquist Court's Pursuit of States' Rights, Color Blind Justice and Mainstream Values," pointed out how courts often "rewrite" Indian law, which has resulted in severe losses to Indian nations' sovereignty and jurisdiction (where tribal courts could make their own decisions).

In 2000, the U.S. Supreme Court handed down decisions in two particular cases that were considered reprehensible in the eyes of Native Americans. One case, *Atkinson Trading Co. v. Shirley,* resulted in the Supreme Court ruling that individual tribes lacked authority to tax non-Indian businesses within their own reservations. The other case, *Nevada v. Hicks,* resulted in the Supreme Court deciding that tribal courts did not have jurisdiction and could not hear cases against non-Indians by Indians, for harms done to them within their reservations.

Lawyers from the Native American Rights Fund (NARF) protested that both rulings were unfair decisions against tribal jurisdiction and sovereignty. To prevent a worsening of this situation and to protect their peoples' rights and sovereignty, tribal leaders in 2001 formed the Tribal Supreme Court Project, which was part of the Tribal Sovereignty Protection Initiative. Its purpose was to unify and strengthen the tribes with a coordinated and consistent approach before the U.S. Supreme Court. Attorneys from NARF and the National Congress of American Indians jointly staff the Tribal Supreme Court Project.

COBELL V. SALAZAR

Other legal issues continue to be at the forefront of courtroom battles for Native American rights. Elouise Cobell has pressed one of those issues. In 1996 Cobell became the lead plaintiff in a class-action lawsuit that the Native American Rights Fund filed against the U.S. government. The suit addressed the more than 300,000 Native Americans who had been swindled out of billions of dollars in royalties owed them by the federal government for oil, gas, and timber, which had been stipulations of the Dawes Act (1887). No tribal member (called "allotees") had ever received a true accounting of their Individual Indian Money (IIM) accounts held in trust by the Department of the Interior's Bureau of Indian Affairs (BIA). When ordered to conduct a true accounting by U.S. District Court Judge Royce Lamberth, the BIA could not do it, so it was nearly impossible to determine how much money individual Indians lost. Secretaries of the interior from Bruce Babbitt to Gale Norton were held in contempt for failing to produce an accounting as ordered. This resulted in the creation of a new department in the Interior Department called the Office of Special Trustee (OST), which now oversees IIM accounts. President Barack Obama's secretary of the interior, Ken Salazar, has been supportive of reaching a settlement. In December 2009, the Obama administration settled the dispute and agreed to disperse more than $3.4 billion to the Native American plaintiffs. Although NARF's attorneys claimed this as a major victory, the money has yet to be received by the Blackfeet people, so the issue remains unsettled.

LANGUAGE AND EDUCATION

It has been said that for people to preserve their culture, they must preserve their language. The Blackfeet people are helping to preserve their culture by teaching their language to the young. Led by Harvard-educated Blackfeet member Darrell Robes Kipp, who runs the Nitsiipowahsin ("Real Speak") School at the Piegan Institute (which was founded in 1987), children in third to eighth grades learn their native language at this immersion school. The Piegan Institute's vision is to "research, promote and preserve Native languages." This effort has increased the number of Blackfeet language speakers. The institute also produces audio and video materials on Blackfeet language and history, and a video about the institute can be found on YouTube. Kipp has produced a book entitled *American Indian Millennium: Renewing Our Ways for Future Generations*; the school has been featured in *Smithsonian Magazine* as well.

Blackfeet people today recognize that one way their children can improve their lives is through education. Blackfeet children attend schools on and off the reservation; after public school, students who show academic promise can avail themselves of grants and aid through a variety of Native American education philanthropies. Two of the most important philanthropies are the American Indian College Fund and the National Indian Education Association, the latter of which is the largest and oldest Indian education organization in the United States.

BLACKFEET IN BUSINESS

The Siyeh Development Corporation is the for-profit corporate arm of the Blackfeet (Amskapi Pikuni) Nation; it is autonomous from the Tribal Council. The corporation owns the Glacier Peaks Casino, Oki Communications (wireless Internet), StarLink Cable, Kimi Bottled Water, and the Blackfeet Heritage Center and Art Gallery. In 2005, Siyeh Development was nominated as a finalist for the John F. Kennedy School of Government Award at Harvard University. The corporation employs more than 150 people, and 60 percent of Siyeh's profits go back to the tribe.

The leasing of lands for oil and natural gas exploration continues, but there is a newer, more renewable source of energy into which the Blackfeet are tapping: wind. Harnessed wind power can provide energy to more than just the Blackfeet Reservation: Besides helping to meet the energy needs of Montana, the Blackfeet wind development project can help with the power needs of surrounding states such as Washington, Oregon, and the Dakotas. Current projects include a wind-powered wastewater treatment plant in Browning, but this is a growing endeavor. The wind project is run by Blackfeet Renewable Energy Inc. and is overseen by

Touring Blackfeet Country

According to the Tourism Department of the Blackfeet Nation, more than 2.3 million people per year visit Glacier National Park, which is next to the reservation (in Canada, visitors can enjoy Waterton Lakes National Park, which shares a border with Glacier National Park). Glacier National Park celebrated its centennial in 2010 (it was founded in 1910). The reservation itself encompasses more than 1.5 million acres, with an average elevation over 4,000 feet (1,220 meters). The Blackfeet Nation's Web site states, "If Montana is the last, best place, the Blackfeet reservation is the best of the best, the last of the last." And visitors can attest to the incredible, dramatic beauty found here, unlike any other place on Earth, with its great diversity of plant and animal life, rugged mountain peaks, and lush plains.

There is something for everyone in Glacier National Park and in the surrounding towns and communities. One of the biggest celebrations of the year is always held during the second week in July—a four-day powwow known as "North American Indian Days," one of the largest gatherings of U.S. and Canadian tribes. History buffs can tour historic places such as Head Smashed-In Buffalo Jump and Running Eagle Falls. For those who like casinos, the reservation is home to Glacier Peaks Casino. The Blackfeet Nation Store in Browning, Montana, is also home to the Blackfeet Heritage Center and Art Gallery, which offers visitors the opportunity to learn more about the traditions and culture of the Blackfeet Nation. Also located in Browning is the Museum of the Plains Indian. Besides showing Blackfeet art, the museum also has displays from other tribes like the Crow, Sioux, Arapaho, and Cree, among others. It contains historic artifacts such as clothing, toys, weapons, and horse gear and is a gallery for contemporary, authentic American Indian arts and crafts. Visitors who desire a more authentic stay can enjoy the amenities at

Lodgepole Gallery and Tipi Village; the gallery displays traditional and contemporary fine art, including Blackfeet art and beadwork. Those who stay at Tipi Village can also enjoy traditional Blackfeet cuisine, tours of historic places such as buffalo jump sites, and horseback-riding trips.

For years, people (both Indian and non-Indian) have protested the lack of any kind of marker to commemorate the site of the Baker (or Bear River) Massacre. In 2007 the Montana Department of Transportation placed a historical marker on Highway 2 a few miles north of the Marias (or Bear) River, and every January 23, people gather at the massacre site to pay their respects to those who died that terrible day in 1870.

Located just outside of Babb, Montana, in the heart of Glacier National Park, is Duck Lake Lodge. Duck Lake has an abundance of fish, and in the winter offers ice fishing, snowmobiling, and skiing. In and around Glacier, there are a number of licensed tribal outfitters; tribal guides can lead visitors on big-game hunts, fishing trips, and other recreational activities. There are also several campgrounds on the reservation, offering visitors fishing, boating, swimming, and tours of Glacier National Park. The Blackfeet Nation Fish and Wildlife Department oversees all activities on the reservation, including big-game hunting, camping, and fishing.

Also in Babb is the world-renowned Babb Bar Cattle Baron Supper Club, owned by Blackfeet tribal members Bob and Charlene Burns. The steakhouse won the 2010 Fastest Disappearing Steak Award from food connoisseur Anthony Bourdain (featured in the May 2010 issue of *Maxim* magazine) as well as other national awards. Besides delicious steak, the supper club features Blackfeet history and culture in its décor and is situated at the border of Many Glacier (part of Glacier National Park).

The Blackfeet Tourism Department doesn't mention one of its greatest treasures, though: the people. With their warmth and generous nature, they make all visitors feel at home.

the federal Division of Energy and Mineral Development office based in Lakewood, Colorado.

POWWOW ETIQUETTE

At modern-day powwows, Native Americans and others gather to dance, sing, socialize, and honor Native American culture. If non-Natives attend a powwow, they should remember that they are guests of another culture and should be appropriately respectful. There is a certain etiquette expected of all who attend powwows, especially visitors. No one should ever touch a part of a dancer's clothing or regalia, for this indicates disrespect. People who want to take video footage or photographs of dancers or other attendees should get permission before doing so.

Visitors should also realize that many special parts of the dancers' or attendees' regalia have been earned and/or have some special meaning. The dance steps also have meaning, and there are usually head dancers for each dance. Some dances are just for men, such as the Grass Dance, and some are just for women, such as the Jingle or Shawl Dances.

Generosity is still part of the Blackfeet tradition, and people are given respect based in part on their generosity to others. During powwows and the annual Indian Days celebrations, everyone is encouraged to give what they can to the drummers, dancers, and singers, as well as to people who have done a great deed such as graduated college or served in the military.

MODERN-DAY WARRIORS

Just as Blackfeet men and women of ancient days served honorably in battling their enemies, they continue to serve the U.S. government today in various uniforms. Blackfeet men and women consider it part of their tradition to serve their country as warriors—according to the tribe's veterans affairs director, Keith Heavy Runner, "Even during peacetime it's about 80 percent of all eligible Blackfeet" who sign up for military service. We're probably

Powwows are large gatherings where people sing, dance, and honor Native American culture. *Above,* a dancer in full regalia during a pow- wow on the Blackfeet Reservation.

in the top 10 of all Indian nations who've served in the military." Wendy Running Crane noted, "Generations of war veterans are in every family."

The Blackfeet people continue to honor those who serve in uniform. The Blackfeet Veterans Affairs Department is commissioning a statue of Minnie Spotted Wolf, who during World War II was the first Native American woman to join the Marine Corps Reserves. Plans are to put the statue at the Plains Museum in Browning, Montana. Today's veterans also serve in the color guard. "This year [2010], for the first time we went to the Tomb of the Unknown Soldier," Heavy Runner said, "and presented the wreath there." The color guard served at the funeral of the last surviving World War I veteran, Frank Buckles, who died in February 2011 at the age of 110.

The veterans who serve as members of the color guard of the Blackfoot Confederacy are, according to Heavy Runner, the "most traveled color guard in the United States," and represent the three other tribes in Canada as well.

The Blackfeet people of today on both sides of the border can feel pride in their accomplishments and in their people as a whole. They have come through terrible times of violence, starvation, disease, poverty, efforts at assimilation, and racism and have not only survived, but are beginning to thrive. They now face a brighter future and know they can take their place in a modern world that finally recognizes their unique place in it.

Chronology

1513–1540	Spanish explorers arrive in what is now the United States, bringing the first horses with them.
1803	The Louisiana Purchase opens western lands to settlers and homesteaders.
1804–1806	Lewis and Clark, with their Corps of Discovery, explore the West.
1820–1830	Trappers disrupt Blackfeet life.
1830–1850s	Smallpox epidemics ravage Blackfeet populations.
1840s	The "Great Emigration" of settlers travels through and settles in traditional Blackfeet lands.
1850	Gold is discovered in the Rocky Mountains.
1851	The Treaty of Fort Laramie is signed.
1855	Lame Bull's Treaty, the first mutually recognized document between the Blackfeet and the U.S. government, is signed.
1860s	The Transcontinental Railroad is constructed; it is completed in 1869.
1860–1885	Buffalo herds dwindle and nearly become extinct due mainly to slaughter by white settlers.
1870	About 200 Piegan are killed as they lay sleeping in what became known as the Bear River (or Marias River) Massacre.
1877	Canada offers Treaty 7 to their Blackfeet, setting aside reserves for them.
1883–1884	The United States fails to provide the Piegan with rations as agreed; more than 600 Piegan die in what becomes known as "Starvation Winter."

1887	The U.S. government takes land from the Blackfeet and restricts them to a smaller reservation.
1887	The Dawes Act, or General Allotment Act, is passed.
1889	Montana gains statehood; more settlers arrive.
1907	The Blackfeet Allotment Act is enacted.
1924	Native Americans are granted U.S. citizenship.
1934	Congress passes the Indian Reorganization Act.
1940s	The U.S. government begins to terminate aid to many Native Americans.
1944	The National Congress of American Indians is formed.
1969–1971	American Indian activists occupy Alcatraz Island in San Francisco Bay for 21 months.
1970	The Native American Rights Fund is founded.

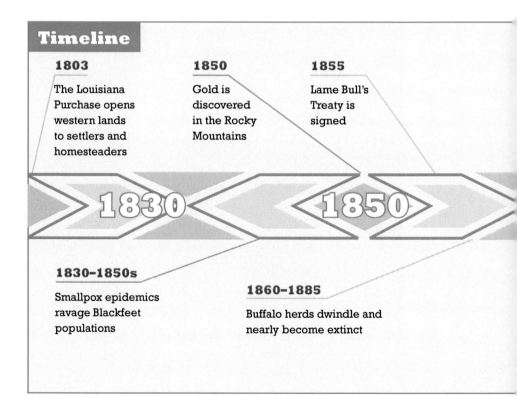

Timeline

1803

The Louisiana Purchase opens western lands to settlers and homesteaders

1850

Gold is discovered in the Rocky Mountains

1855

Lame Bull's Treaty is signed

1830   1850

1830–1850s

Smallpox epidemics ravage Blackfeet populations

1860–1885

Buffalo herds dwindle and nearly become extinct

1974	Blackfeet Community College is founded.
1975	The Indian Self-Determination and Education Assistance Act is passed.
1989 & 1991	The University of Lethbridge in Alberta publishes the first Blackfeet grammar book and dictionary.
1990	The Indian Arts and Crafts Act is passed, to protect and promote authentic Native American-made items.
1990	The Native American Graves Protection and Repatriation Act is signed by President George H.W. Bush.
2009	*Cobell v. Salazar* is finally settled; as of this writing, however, no money has yet been awarded to the allottees.
2010	The Blackfeet people debate the creation of a new constitution.

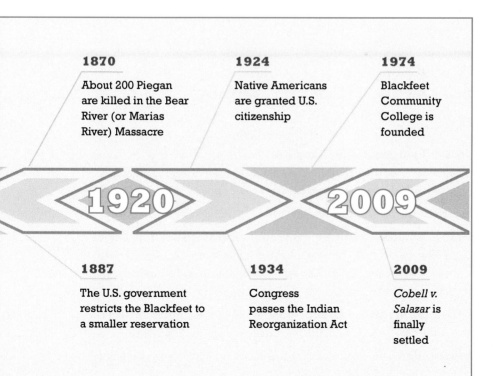

1870

About 200 Piegan are killed in the Bear River (or Marias River) Massacre

1924

Native Americans are granted U.S. citizenship

1974

Blackfeet Community College is founded

1920   **2009**

1887

The U.S. government restricts the Blackfeet to a smaller reservation

1934

Congress passes the Indian Reorganization Act

2009

Cobell v. Salazar is finally settled

Glossary

agent A person appointed by the Bureau of Indian Affairs to supervise U.S. government programs on a reservation and/or in a specific region.

anthropologist A scientist who studies human beings and their culture.

archaeologist A scientist who studies the material remains of past human cultures.

band A loosely organized group of people bound together by the need for food and defense, by family ties and/or other common interests.

Bureau of Indian Affairs (BIA) A federal government agency, now within the Department of the Interior, founded to manage relations with Native American tribes.

clan An affiliation from birth, often associated with the mother's or father's clan.

culture The learned behavior of humans; socially taught activities; the way of life of a people.

Dawes Act Enacted in 1887, the act provided for the division of tribally held lands into individually owned parcels and the opening up of "surplus" lands to resettlement by non-Indians.

Indian Reorganization Act (IRA) Enacted in 1934, this legislation provided some relief to the Blackfeet. It was a start at protecting tribal lands and the sovereignty of tribal governments.

matrilineal Relating to descent or kinship through the female line.

Native American Graves Protection and Repatriation Act of 1990 A law that allows Native American tribes to repossess the artifacts and grave remains that were taken from them by museums and individual collectors.

O-kan (or Medicine Lodge) Dance The annual major ceremonial rite of the Blackfeet. It is also often referred to as the Sun Dance.

repatriation The return of human remains, funerary objects, and other artifacts to their rightful ancestral owners.

reservation   Land set aside for American Indians on the basis of treaties.

shaman   A spiritual leader.

sovereignty   A nation or state's supreme power within its borders.

treaty   A legal and binding document by which two opposing parties make an agreement.

tribe   A society consisting of separate communities united by culture, family ties, religion, and other interests.

vision quest   A four-day fast usually performed alone by the young. The vision they saw would be their personal "medicine," or guardian.

Bibliography

Axline, Jon, and Glenda Clay Bradshaw. *Montana's Historical Highway Markers.* Helena: Montana Historical Society Press, 2008.

Brandon, William. *Indians.* Boston: Houghton Mifflin and Company, 1989.

Cantor, George. *North American Indian Landmarks: A Traveler's Guide.* London: Visible Ink Press, 1993.

Claiborne, Robert. *The Emergence of Man: The First Americans.* New York: Time-Life Books, 1973.

Deloria, Philip J., et al. *The Native Americans: An Illustrated History.* Atlanta: Turner Publishing, 1993.

Ewers, John. *The Blackfeet: Raiders on the Northwestern Plains.* Norman: University of Oklahoma Press, 1988.

Freedman, Russell. *Indian Chiefs.* New York: Holiday House, 1987.

Getches, David H. "Beyond Indian Law: The Rehnquist Court's Pursuit of States' Rights, Color-Blind Justice, and Mainstream Values," *Minnesota Law Review* 86, 2001.

Green, Rayna. *Women in American Indian Society.* New York: Chelsea House Publishers, 1992.

Heinemann, Sue. *Amazing Women in American History: A Book of Answers for Kids.* New York: John Wiley & Sons, 1998.

Hungry Wolf, Adolf. *The Blackfoot Papers: Volume IV, Pikunni Biographies.* Skookumchuck, British Columbia, Canada: Good Medicine Cultural Foundation, 2006.

Hungry Wolf, Dorothy. *The Ways of My Grandmothers.* New York: William Morrow and Co., 1980.

Kelly, Lawrence C. *Federal Indian Policy.* New York: Chelsea House Publishers, 1990.

Kipp, Woody. *Viet Cong at Wounded Knee: The Trail of a Blackfeet Activist.* Norman: University of Oklahoma Press, 2008.

Lacey, T. Jensen. *The Blackfeet.* New York: Chelsea House, 2005.

Lovett, Haley A. "Happy Birthday, Abraham Maslow, Father of the Hierarchy of Needs." FindingDulcinea.com. April 1, 2010. Accessed July 19,

2010. Available online. URL: http://www.findingdulcinea.com/features/ profiles/m/abraham-maslow.html.

Mails, Thomas E. *The Mystic Warriors of the Plains.* New York: Doubleday & Co., 1972.

_____. *Plains Indians: Dog Soldiers, Bear Men, and Buffalo Women.* New York: Bonanza Books, 1973.

Matthiessen, Peter. *Indian Country.* New York: Viking Press, 1984.

McFee, Malcolm. *Modern Blackfeet: Montanans on a Reservation.* Long Grove, Ill.: Waveland Press, 1984.

Nies, Judith. *Native American History: A Chronology of a Culture's Vast Achievements and Their Links to World Events.* New York: Ballantine Books, 1996.

Niethammer, Carolyn. *Daughters of the Earth: The Lives and Legends of American Indian Women.* New York: Collier Books, 1977.

Oldershaw, Barbara (1987). "Blackfeet American Indian Women: Builders of the Tribe." *Places,* 4(1), 38. Retrieved from: http://escholarship.org/ uc/item/0s58p2fc on May 15, 2010.

Powers, William K. *Indian Dancing and Costumes.* New York: G. P. Putnam's Sons, 1966.

Rosier, Paul C., Ph.D. "'They Are Ancestral Homelands': Race, Place, and Politics in Cold War Native America, 1945–1961." *The Journal of American History,* March 2006, pp. 1300–1326.

_____. *Rebirth of the Blackfeet Nation 1912–1954.* Lincoln: University of Nebraska Press, 2001.

Samek, Hana. "The Blackfoot Confederacy, 1880–1920: A Comparative Study of Canadian and U.S. Indian Policy." *American Indian Quarterly,* Vol. 13 No. 3: 286–288. University of Nebraska Press.

Spencer, Robert F., and Jesse D. Jennings, et al. *The Native Americans.* New York: Harper & Row, 1977.

Staeger, Rob. *Native American Religions.* Philadelphia: Mason Crest Publishers, 2003.

Welch, James T. *Fools Crow.* New York: Viking Penguin, 1986.

Williams, Colleen Madonna Flood. *Native American Family Life.* Philadelphia: Mason Crest Publishers, 2003.

Further Resources

Books

Bullchild, Percy. *The Sun Came Down: The History of the World as My Blackfeet Elders Told It.* Lincoln: University of Nebraska Press, 2005.

Grinnell, George Bird. *Blackfeet Indian Stories.* Helena, Mont.: Riverbend Publishing, 2005.

McClintock, Walter. *The Old North Trail: Life, Legends, and Religion of the Blackfeet Indian.* Lincoln: University of Nebraska Press, 1999.

Wischmann, Lesley. *Frontier Diplomats: Alexander Culbertson and Natoyist-Siksina Among the Blackfeet.* Norman: University of Oklahoma Press, 2004.

Web Sites

American Indian College Fund
http://www.collegefund.org

American Indian Education Foundation
http://www.aiefprograms.org

American Indian Movement
http://www.aimovement.org

Americans for Indian Opportunity
http://www.aio.org

Blackfeet Constitutional Reform
http://www.blackfeetvoice.org

Blackfeet Nation
http://blackfeetnation.com

Four Directions Teaching
http://fourdirectionsteachings.com

Gathering of Nations
http://www.gatheringofnations.com

Good Medicine Cultural Foundation
http://www.goodmedicinefoundation.com

Head Smashed-In Buffalo Jump Interpretive Center
http://www.head-smashed-in.com

The Institute for Tribal Government
http://www.tribalgov.pdx.edu/

National Congress of American Indians
http://www.ncai.org

National Indian Education Association
http://www.niea.org

National Museum of the American Indian
http://www.nmai.si.edu

Native American Online
http://www.native-american-online.org

Native American Rights Fund
http://www.narf.org

Native Arts & Cultures Foundation
http://www.nativeartsandcultures.org

The Piegan Institute
http://www.pieganinstitute.org

Town of Browning, Montana
http://www.browningmontana.com

Picture Credits

Index

About the Contributors

T. JENSEN LACEY is freelance journalist, photographer, and author of more than 700 articles for newspapers and magazines. A contributor to the *Chicken Soup for the Soul* books, she has published eight other books, including *The Comanche* in Chelsea House's The History and Culture of Native Americans set. Lacey is of Comanche, Cherokee, and Seneca descent, a charter member of the National Museum of the American Indian, and a member of Western Writers of America.

Series editor **PAUL C. ROSIER** received his Ph.D. in American History from the University of Rochester in 1998. Dr. Rosier currently serves as Associate Professor of History at Villanova University (Villanova, Pennsylvania), where he teaches Native American History, American Environmental History, Global Environmental Justice Movements, History of American Capitalism, and World History.

In 2001, the University of Nebraska Press published his first book, *Rebirth of the Blackfeet Nation, 1912–1954;* in 2003, Greenwood Press published *Native American Issues* as part of its Contemporary Ethnic American Issues series. In 2006, he coedited an international volume called *Echoes from the Poisoned Well: Global Memories of Environmental Injustice*. Dr. Rosier has also published articles in the *American Indian Culture and Research Journal,* the *Journal of American Ethnic History,* and *The Journal of American History.* His *Journal of American History* article, entitled "They Are Ancestral Homelands: Race, Place, and Politics in Cold War Native America, 1945–1961," was selected for inclusion in *The Ten Best History Essays of 2006–2007,* published by Palgrave MacMillan in 2008; and it won the Western History Association's 2007 Arrell Gibson Award for Best Essay on the history of Native Americans. His latest book, *Serving Their Country: American Indian Politics and Patriotism in the Twentieth Century* (Harvard University Press), is winner of the 2010 Labriola Center American Indian National Book Award.

Acknowledgments

Special thanks to Wendy Running Crane, Keith Heavy Runner, Woody Kipp, and other tribal members who were such a help in creating this book. Thanks also to proofreaders Marian Jensen, Cheryl Sansom, Eric Lacey, and Patricia Edmundson.